NEW MEXICO
THEN & NOW

CONTEMPORARY REPHOTOGRAPHY BY
WILLIAM STONE

PREFACE BY
WILLIAM STONE

ESSAYS AND AFTERWORD BY
JEROLD WIDDISON

William Stone
Bowdoin - Class of 1978

WESTCLIFFE PUBLISHERS

westcliffepublishers.com

CONTENTS

Photographers have been drawn to New Mexico for a hundred and fifty years. They have come for the unique features of the land and for the layered history of its people. And they have come for the light—a light that seems at times preternatural; transformed by the interplay of terrain and atmosphere, it infuses the landscape with qualities seldom equaled elsewhere.

These attractions of New Mexico were discovered early. Many of the first photographers to work in New Mexico were participating in government or railroad exploratory expeditions to the West. Still others sought to earn a living by photographing the people or the land and selling their images to visitors and residents alike. Then later—in the early decades of the twentieth century—several photographers involved in their medium's entry into the realm of fine art did important work here.

The photographers of long ago indeed left a precious record for us—a visual journal of people, places, and events that have shaped New Mexico. Their early-day photographs portray a land diverse in its heritage. Frontier military forts and Indian trading posts, mining boomtowns and lumbering camps, early railroads and wagon trails, prehistoric archaeological sites and Indian pueblos, main-street businesses and village churches, layered sandstone escarpments and isolated volcanic monoliths—all are subjects that were pictured by early-day photographers working in New Mexico.

These old photographs have the unique ability to transport viewers back to the instant when the photographers captured for posterity the scenes laid out before their cameras. This ability of photography to reverse time—even if for only a moment—is part of its magic. While allowing us to step back in time, old photographs also invite us to question what has happened through the years to the places pictured long ago, and to wonder how the same scenes look today.

This is the premise behind *New Mexico: Then & Now*. By pairing historical photographs of New Mexico scenes with identically composed, modern-day images shot from the same camera locations —the technique of repeat photography—we are inviting readers to make their own side-by-side comparisons of time-separated views. Some of these scenes have changed dramatically, others little. In either case, the comparisons can speak volumes about what has

JOURNEYS IN TIME AND PLACE

Welcome Sign, Arizona–New Mexico Line on US 66, 1940

happened in these places during the intervening years, and perhaps even prompt speculation about what the future holds.

Inspiration for this book stems from recent work by Colorado's preeminent landscape photographer, John Fielder, and his company, Westcliffe Publishers. Together they produced *Colorado: 1870–2000*, which matched historical photographs by William Henry Jackson with John's modern-day repeat photographs of the same subjects, all presented in an elegant and immensely popular book. Seeing the widespread interest in a book based on repeat photography, John and Westcliffe decided to produce similar books about other western states. Since I had previously worked on two New Mexico books with Westcliffe, they offered the project of photographing *New Mexico: Then & Now* to me. With little delay, I excitedly accepted the offer.

That was a little over two years—and many thousands of driving miles—ago. Since then my photographic journeys have taken me throughout my adopted home state—from the Four Corners to Carlsbad Caverns, from the Bootheel to the Sangre de Cristo Mountains, from White Sands to Toltec Gorge, and to countless places in between—all in an effort to see, and to document, how New Mexico *now* compares with New Mexico *then*.

≈ ≈ ≈ ≈

My work on *New Mexico: Then & Now* began with a quest for historical photographs that would collectively form the "then" view of the state. I quickly discovered that the photo archive at the Museum of New Mexico's Palace of the Governors in Santa Fe is the mother lode of historical New Mexico photography. Broadening my search, I also found many other entities that collect old pictures,

and I have included here photographs from the collections of history and art museums, universities, libraries, historical societies, federal agencies, and individuals.

Because no single early-day photographer had pictured New Mexico with the broad-ranging coverage needed to fully tell the story, I selected photographs made by many photographers. In fact, I have included historical images made by more than forty named photographers and by nearly as many whose names have become separated from their work over the years.

In selecting the historical photographs, I had several goals in mind. First and foremost, I hoped to create a set that would present a comprehensive view of the varied layers of New Mexico's story. And, while I knew that readers would expect to see well-known subjects like Santa Fe's Palace of the Governors, Albuquerque's Old Town, Taos Pueblo, and the Rio Grande, I also felt strongly about including a few surprises. Consequently, I went to considerable effort to find and photograph little-known scenes such as the Giants of the Mimbres, the view from Mesa Chivato, the U.S.-Mexico boundary in the Bootheel, and Todilto Park north of Gallup.

I also thought the book would be more interesting and thought-provoking if the then-and-now comparisons evidenced a broad range of change through the years, and I believe they do. Another goal of my search was to include subjects from throughout the state. And although I was generally able to achieve this, I did come up short in finding suitable old photographs of New Mexico's eastern plains, an area that is underrepresented here.

"The older, the better" was the primary theme guiding my selection process; I wanted the span between "then" and "now" to be as long as possible. I was pleasantly surprised to find many fine images from the 1860s, '70s, and '80s, and even one from about 1855 —the oldest included here, a view from the Santa Fe Plaza (see p. 14).

As my collection of potentially rephotographable old scenes of New Mexico took shape, I began working on logistical and technical issues—finding the field locations of the old photos; finding out whether I would need permission to photograph here or there; deciding on specific camera equipment to use; and determining the photographically optimal time of day, season, or lighting conditions for each scene.

Over the years, my personal adventuring and photographic endeavors—as well as my professional work as a geodesist for the National Geodetic Survey—have taken me throughout New Mexico. Because of my time in the field, I have a broad familiarity with the state that, along with a bit of literature and map research, would usually allow me to figure out where old photograph subjects were located. Some of the old photographs that interested me, however, were of places I had never previously visited, while still others depicted scenes completely unknown to me. Discovering some of these places was among the experiential highlights of my work on the project.

As I began visiting the places pictured in the old images, the photo subjects of long ago started coming to life for me. Stories, both old and new, began surfacing. Some of the stories were about the places, while others were about their inhabitants. Some of the stories emerged from my own research, while others—often my favorites—evolved out of personal encounters on the road.

I will likely never forget the hospitality of the Martinez family, for example. I met them at the 2002 biennial Dawson town reunion. All twelve Martinez siblings were delivered by the same company doctor in Dawson, where their father had worked the coal mines. During my time with the family at their campsite near the old Dawson cemetery, I was regaled with tales of what life was like more than fifty years ago in this company-owned coal town, now long abandoned.

In the border town of Columbus, I met Richard Dean, great-grandson of James T. Dean, one of the victims of Pancho Villa's 1916 raid on Columbus. Dick possesses a wealth of knowledge about the area's history, which he generously shared with me. He even helped facilitate a couple of my repeat photographs. Dick and his wife, Betty, graciously welcomed me into their home during my visits to Columbus.

At Trinity Site, I met Ben Benjamin. As a young army sergeant in 1945, Ben witnessed the explosion of the world's first atomic bomb from his observation bunker only six miles away—as close to Ground Zero as anyone was allowed. Ben was responsible for operating cameras and other monitoring instruments during the blast. As the mushroom cloud rose into the sky, Ben, watching through dark-filtered glass, exclaimed to his boss, "My God, it's beautiful!" To which his boss replied, "No, it's terrible." Both men were probably right.

It is because of such stories—of both history and experience—that I chose to describe each image with a lengthy caption, although all the stories are worthy of even greater detail than page space allows. My hope is that readers will find the photographs—old and new—interesting in their own right, and that the captions will simply help elucidate details of the scenes pictured and the process of picturing them.

In all this I am reminded of something written by Sam Abell, a photographer and uniquely gifted teacher of my acquaintance. In eloquently describing the connection between photography and story in *Sam Abell: The Photographic Life*, he states, "Seeking the picture is the complex process that dominates documentary photography, and in the seeking there is often a story. The story varies. At its best it is magical; at its worst it is bitterly frustrating—you see the picture, but can't get to it."

Indeed, I experienced both magic and frustration as I worked on this book. The magical part came in the form of the successful photographs, most of the people that I met, and the places that I experienced. The frustration had many faces as well—the lighting was no good, I couldn't find the camera location, the scene was compromised by clutter or trash, there were too many trees blocking the view, or I was unable to get permission to photograph a proprietary scene. In fact, some of my photography excursions netted not a single publishable image; things just didn't come together for me. But ultimately, even the failures—the frustration part of the process that Sam speaks of—added to the base of knowledge and experience that I carried with me on the next trip.

After all, even William Henry Jackson, perhaps the most important and skilled photographer of the early West, met with catastrophic failure during an 1877 expedition through the Southwest. He had brought with him a newly introduced dry film, which would allow him to leave behind his cumbersome wet-plate negatives, chemicals, and portable darkroom. He later discovered that the film—all four hundred sheets—was defective, and all of the trip's photographic work, including what would have been the first photographs of the great prehistoric ruins at Chaco Canyon, was for naught. Fifty-nine years later, at age ninety-three, Jackson once again visited Chaco and hiked the steep trail to Pueblo Alto, a mesa-top site that he had discovered during his photographically disastrous visit.

Photographer William Stone

Photograph by Carolyn Stone

❧ ❧ ❧ ❧

Repeat photography—or rephotography, as it is also known—is the process of locating the site of an existing photograph and shooting a new photograph of the same scene from the original camera location. It is a powerful tool for studying visible change over time, and it is just as well-suited for rigorous scientific studies as it is for general-interest comparisons. And although I find unsettling the idea of copying someone else's photographs, repeat photography pursues a goal higher than the rote duplication of another's vision—it is to facilitate a comparison of the "then" with the "now" and perhaps to prompt mindfulness about the changes.

Practitioners of technical repeat photography attain image-matching specificity by duplicating not only the camera location of the original photograph, but the season and sun position as well. They make measurements on a test photograph, exposed on instant film, from their initial estimate of the camera location, and compare these image dimensions with the corresponding measurements on the historical photograph—all in order to fine-tune their camera location. I admire—and enjoy doing—such technical exercises.

However, my primary photographic interest is the scenic landscape, and the quality of the light gracing my images is paramount. I decided at the outset of this project that I would forgo some of the details of technical repeat photography—such as season and sun-position matching—and would instead adopt a hybrid approach, a compromise between repeat photography and scenic photography. (One notable exception is my photograph of the Luna County

Courthouse, for which I precisely matched the time of day on the clock tower.) Quite simply, I wanted my "now" photographs to match their "then" counterparts as closely as possible, but I also felt strongly that my shots should have their own scenic quality.

And, although I usually chose good lighting over matched time of day or season, I did work diligently in determining the original photographers' camera vantage points. When scenes included detailed structure in the foreground that I could use—such as identifiable rocks—along with foreground-to-background relationships, I was able to position my camera within inches of the original camera location. My reshoots of Fort Cummings, Toltec Gorge, and Cubero, to name a few, include the kind of foreground detail needed for this degree of location-matching precision. For other scenes, those with only distant features and very little in the foreground to help, it was impossible to make camera setups with as much certainty.

On several occasions in the field, when I knew I was zeroing in on my goal of finding a camera location, I would spot a rock outcrop or some other natural elevation, just the kind of place I'm always seeking out to set up the tripod for my own scenic shots. I'd climb up on it, compare all the details of the photograph with the scene before me, and smile—knowing I had found the precise spot. Times

William H. Jackson with his camera, Laguna Pueblo, late 1800s

like this were very satisfying and exciting—both because I had identified the camera location and because of the connection I felt with the early photographer who, generations earlier and from the very same place, had made the photograph I held in my hand.

When the view from the desired camera location was obscured—perhaps by trees, a situation I encountered throughout my travels—or when the spot fell in the middle of a now-busy street, I shifted the camera enough to attain a clearer view or a safer vantage point. Early on in the project, I purchased a twelve-foot-tall tripod, which saved several shots by allowing me to position my camera above view-blocking obstructions.

Determining the camera location, however, was not always enough to get the shot I wanted. Sometimes conditions for photography were just not right—there were too many dark shadows, or the sky was too cloudy or too boring, or it was too windy, or I missed the good light because I had to change a flat tire. I got lucky on rare occasions and was able to get my shot—with nice light—during my first visit to a site. For some photographs, I made several tries (a half-dozen or more in a few cases) to get good conditions. Included here are a few repeat images for which I never did get the photographic look that I was after—these shots frustrated me right to the end. And the locations of a handful of the old scenes eluded me. One in particular, an 1884 view of some wonderful pedestal rocks in western New Mexico, will continue to prey on my thoughts until I find the place, which I will—someday!

Repeat photography involves a completely different picture-taking strategy than traditional scenic photography. When I venture out to do scenic photography, I usually have in mind a general idea of the subjects I want to shoot, and I will fine-tune my game plan based on the evolving lighting conditions.

I recall Dewitt Jones, another photographer and impassioned teacher, offering photographic advice during a workshop many years ago. He said that if you go out to shoot fall color, for instance, but Mother Nature happens to be making rainbows that day, shoot the rainbows instead—a simply worded nugget of photographic wisdom that I have carried with me for years. But such flexibility is not allowed in repeat photography. The camera location and composition have already been decided, and the only freedom is to choose when and under what conditions to photograph.

This disparity between repeat and traditional photography was borne out on several occasions as I traveled New Mexico. While I was photographing Navajo Church, the partially clouded eastern sky was suddenly set afire by the rising sun, but my repeat shot was looking to the west. Shooting at the Giants of the Mimbres, some of the most dramatic storm clouds I have seen in years closed in just before an intense double rainbow appeared, but opposite from the direction of my shot. At Lincoln, a nearly full moon rose above the town just before sunset, but it was positioned a few lunar diameters off the edge of my repeat-photo frame.

In each of these situations, and others like them, I really wanted to photograph the "rainbows," to borrow Dewitt's idea, because that's what Mother Nature was making at the time. But instead I shot the "fall color" because that was the subject I needed for this book. The truth be told, sometimes I was able to get both.

≈   ≈   ≈   ≈

In *Burntwater*, a fine little book of essays on the Southwest, Scott Thybony discusses the setting of Ansel Adams' photograph "Moonrise, Hernandez, New Mexico," which was made in 1941. In examining how the scene of this dramatic and acclaimed photograph has changed in a half-century, Scott says, "Hernandez has aged, grown more complex over the years. New layers have accumulated on top of the old. A highway maintenance shed partially screens the adobe church from view. Metal has reshaped its roofline, and a chain-link fence encloses the cemetery. But beyond the village, the mountains and the vast sky still wait for another moonrise."

It is true that Adams' view of Hernandez can no longer be rephotographed, or even seen clearly. Yet Scott's description struck me as so perfect and so applicable to many of the scenes that I did rephotograph. Many places in New Mexico have been altered by the accumulation of "layers," new on top of old. But regardless of how much new has come along, something of the old is usually found peeking through. That, to me, is part of the charm of the Land of Enchantment. For in spite of all the changes that have occurred, the settings of many of these scenes appear much the same today as they did years ago. Indeed, these places still wait for yet another moonrise.

Santa Fe is by far the oldest capital city in the United States. Founded between 1607 and 1610 as the seat of government for the remote Spanish colony of *Nuevo México*, it remains today the capital of the forty-seventh state of the United States, New Mexico.

Not that the settlement was thought of as a city, much less a capital, in its early days. It was the *Villa de Santa Fé*, "villa" being the appropriate term for a governing outpost of Spain's empire.

The Villa was a very small settlement. For more than a century, in fact, it was the *only* Spanish settlement in New Mexico. The initial purpose of the colony was to Christianize the Pueblo Indians, which required dedicated missionary friars in the pueblos, not citizen settlers in villages or towns. New Mexico was then but a minor offshoot of the real Mexico, Spain's much more productive colony centered at Mexico City.

Furthermore, Santa Fe was two thousand miles from Mexico City—far to the north, beyond many mountains and deserts. A caravan of supply was sent out to Santa Fe only once every three years, which was almost the time needed for a round trip. Several of New Mexico's royal governors, therefore, expressed their disgust with the place, one cautiously writing to his king that Santa Fe was "remote beyond compare."

Santa Fe in those times was peopled only by the custodian of the Catholic friars, several families as needed to maintain the Villa, a few royal soldiers, a number of already-Christianized Indian servants from Mexico, and of course the king's governor and captain general, who held forth in the rambling adobe structure known today as the Palace of the Governors. All other buildings, including a church, were also made of adobe and were clustered around the Plaza.

For nearly two hundred fifty years Santa Fe continued thus. To be sure, a hiatus of twelve years occurred from 1680 when the Pueblo Indians rose in revolt, killing the friars and driving the other Spaniards entirely out of New Mexico. But when the Spaniards returned in reconquest, it was with an understanding that they had better consolidate their power with additional settlements and people. It was for this reason that the other Hispanic towns and villages of New Mexico were founded.

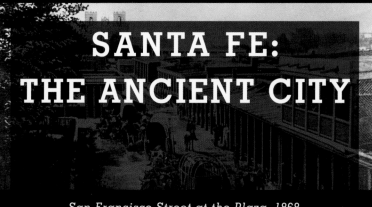

SANTA FE: THE ANCIENT CITY

San Francisco Street at the Plaza, 1868

The year 1821 also brought a degree of change, as Mexico won independence from Spain. New Mexico became a province of the new republic, though no less remote. Nevertheless, the collapse of royal control allowed Anglo-American traders and merchants to establish the Santa Fe Trail, reaching from Franklin, Missouri, to Santa Fe. Every summer, several hundred wagonloads of merchandise were brought over the trail to supply the people of Santa Fe and New Mexico with goods they had never had before.

Then after New Mexico and Upper California were won for the United States in the Mexican War of 1846–1848, things began to change more rapidly. More Anglo-Americans from the Midwestern and Eastern states arrived, bringing with them more goods, tools, skills, and energies, along with new ways of life and thinking.

Among them were several practitioners of the art and science of photography. How eager these men were to picture the landscapes, the peoples, and the curiosities of the strange new territory they entered. Most of them came over the trail directly to Santa Fe, and their surviving photographs provide a surprisingly complete record of the Villa's old buildings, together with a good sense of the overall appearance, size, and character of the adobe town and of its inhabitants.

Santa Fe soon came to have several Victorian-style buildings, as well as adobe buildings made over into something called Territorial style—a simplified version of the Greek Revival style that was already passé in the eastern United States. How full of contrast the "urban" scene became: Gilded Age hotels, tall mansard-roofed schools, and Greek-detailed houses rising amid adobe, dust, and mud.

In 1885, an ungainly three-story capitol building (below) was erected, across the Santa Fe River from the historic Plaza and the Palace of the Governors. Many in town hated the building, and soon it burned—quite suspiciously. That capitol was succeeded by another on the same site, and, in 1966, by still another nearby.

In the early 1900s another change in the appearance of the city began: a conscious return to the past known as the Pueblo Revival style of architecture. Many buildings took on the adobe look that had earlier been eschewed, although they were now more studied and finished-looking than the oldest adobe structures. The Pueblo Revival style—now also called Santa Fe style—was rooted both in romanticism and in calculated efforts to maintain Santa Fe's exotic appeal for tourists.

Today, Santa Fe is still remarkable for its mixture of the ancient and the modern. Life is indeed slower here, Spanish and Indian languages are heard in the narrow streets, and the streets themselves still dwindle off into the piñon-covered hills as in days of yore.

The historical photos of the Villa on these pages are only a sampling, yet they may be enough to point up something that differentiates Santa Fe from most other cities and towns of the American West: When photography was new, Santa Fe was old.

≋　≋　≋　≋

First Territorial Capitol, circa 1890 (see p. 10)

The Palace of the Governors is a perfect expression of the history of Santa Fe. From the earliest days of the Villa until nearly the present, this oldest public building in the United States has served every changing need of government and has been modified to reflect every architectural style in vogue. At first the thick-walled adobe compound contained the *casas reales*, the royal houses of the Spanish governors: offices, living quarters, workrooms, storage rooms, and stables. During the 1680 revolt of the Pueblos, its walls sheltered the beleaguered colonists, who soon fought their way out to flee down the Rio Grande with their livestock. A dozen years later, when the Spaniards returned in force, the building was reworked and again made the seat of government.

A century and a half later, the Palace was taken over by American military and territorial governors, with a few rooms fitted up for a territorial legislature—something unheard of in Spanish times. "The adobe palace," as the building was rather disrespectfully called during this time, was described as having a "primitive appearance . . . the roof supported by great pine beams, blackened and stained by age . . . the floors earthen . . . the woodwork heavy and rough. . . ." Rooms and alcoves were reused for a post office, library, surveyor's office, and jail.

Soon a *portal*, or portico, of sawn lumber was added along the front (opposite page, left), and in time the portico was given a more refined and Gothic look, with an upper railing of decorative spindles.

View of Santa Fe from Fort Marcy Hill, circa 1900 (see pp. 8–9)

But when influential proponents of romanticism and nativism arrived and insisted that Santa Fe architecture mimic the style of Indian pueblos, the all-wood *portal* of the Palace was replaced by one in the Pueblo Revival style, much as it appears today.

By the late 1880s the Palace was finally outworn as the seat of New Mexico's government. Governor and legislature moved to the disliked new capitol, and the Palace itself became the territory's first historical museum.

✵ ✵ ✵ ✵

Appearing in this book (on p. 14) is one of the oldest known photographs of Santa Fe, a circa 1855 view from the southeastern corner of the Plaza, where the Santa Fe Trail reached its destination. What is not known, however, is the identity of the picture maker.

As for photographers of Santa Fe who *are* known, among the earliest to arrive were Nicholas Brown and his son William Henry Brown. The two opened a studio near the Plaza in 1866 and continued in business there for several years. Making portraits of army officers and of individuals and families was probably their main line of work, though they also took pictures of local buildings and street scenes. That they sought everyone's business is obvious, for they advertised in both English and Spanish, and certainly their work in Santa Fe provided experience for the younger Brown, who later had studios in the Mexican cities of Chihuahua and Parral. In any event, two old photographs by Nicholas Brown are reproduced in these pages: the Palace of the Governors (opposite) and the old *Parroquia*, Santa Fe's parish church (see p. 11).

In the summers of 1873 and 1874, several photographs of Santa Fe scenes were made by Timothy H. O'Sullivan (1840–1882), then a photographer for the Wheeler Geographical Surveys of the Territories. Although the surveys' primary interest in New Mexico was mapmaking and the evaluation of natural resources, O'Sullivan and his camera could hardly ignore the archaic buildings and appearance of the old Villa—witness his picture on page 12 of San Miguel Church.

Several other photographers made pictures in and around the city in the last years of the 1800s and the first years of the 1900s, including William Henry Jackson, J. R. Riddle, and Christian Kaadt. Then in the second decade of the 1900s, a good many photographs

Construction of St. Francis of Assisi Cathedral around La Parroquia, 1880s (see p. 11)

were made by two men who were especially devoted to Santa Fe and all of northern New Mexico—Jesse Nusbaum and T. Harmon Parkhurst.

Nusbaum (1887–1975), who became the first staff member of the Museum of New Mexico when it was established and installed in the Palace in 1912, was an archaeologist who eventually served three times as superintendent of Mesa Verde National Park. Long a Santa Fe enthusiast and a leading light of the community, Nusbaum was interested in everything and took pictures of almost everything.

T. Harmon Parkhurst arrived in Santa Fe from New York state in 1910. He was hired as photographer at the museum not long after its founding, and about 1915 he opened his own studio and photo business. A versatile and prolific photographer for years, he also made pictures of nearly everything in Santa Fe and traveled widely about northern New Mexico, doing good work with all kinds of subject matter. Little is remembered about Parkhurst aside from his photographs, but he was likely among the first in New Mexico to use an automobile for getting around in search of pictures— what a change that was from the oxen and covered wagons of Nicholas Brown's time!

Palace of the Governors, 1868

Santa Fe's Palace of the Governors is the oldest public building in the United States. It was built in 1610— only a dozen years after the establishment of San Gabriel, New Mexico's first European settlement. Although never actually a palace in a traditional sense, the building served as the governmental seat during New Mexico's days of Spanish and Mexican rule and for the first four decades of its U.S. territorial period. Also, for twelve years following the Pueblo Revolt of 1680, Indian leaders occupied the complex. Seven years before this photograph was made, the Confederate flag flew briefly over the Palace of the Governors during the Civil War. The tall poles seen here are for wires of the recently arrived telegraph.

The Palace of the Governors has undergone a number of renovations and architectural transformations during its nearly four centuries of existence. In its earlier days, the complex was considerably larger than it is today. The walled and fortified compound reportedly could at one time hold more than a thousand people, five thousand head of sheep and goats, four hundred horses and mules, and three hundred head of beef cattle—without crowding. The Palace's most recent major renovation, completed in 1913, converted the structure's architectural style from Territorial (seen in the historical photograph) to Pueblo Revival. On most days, vendors line the sidewalk beneath the Palace's portal and display their wares to the strolling crowds.

These two abutting photographs by Timothy H. O'Sullivan provide a fine, sweeping view of Santa Fe from the original, although never garrisoned, hilltop site of Fort Marcy. Among the identifiable structures in these images are, from the left, La Parroquia, Santa Fe's parish church, built in 1710; the Plaza and its 1868 war memorial; the Palace of the Governors; the Guadalupe Church; the quarters and parade ground of Fort Marcy; and the partially constructed federal building, at the far right. Note the large agricultural fields stretching from near Palace Avenue to the foot of the hill.

It's difficult to imagine that this is the same scene that O'Sullivan photographed almost a hundred and thirty years earlier (also see p. 6). Buildings and trees have taken over Santa Fe. Working across the images, from the left we see St. Francis of Assisi Cathedral, which replaced La Parroquia *in the 1880s; the Bataan Building, with its prominent tower on the skyline; La Fonda Hotel, in line with the Bataan Building; the site of the Plaza, completely hidden in the trees; Guadalupe Church; El Dorado Hotel; and the U.S. Courthouse site, hidden in the trees (the federal building was finally completed in 1889, thirty-six years after construction began).*

Second Territorial Capitol, circa 1905

Bataan Memorial Building

New Mexico's second capitol building was erected in 1900 on the same site as the first territorial capitol (see p. 5). The earlier building had been completed in 1885, well south of Santa Fe's Plaza and the Palace of the Governors, after local authorities decided that the Palace was hopelessly inadequate for further territorial government use. However, the massive stone structure burned down only seven years after its construction. Its successor, above, generally adhered to the Greek Revival style popular in American public buildings of the era. In 1912, after several unsuccessful attempts, New Mexico gained statehood, and this building became the first state capitol of the forty-seventh state.

In the early 1950s, the state capitol underwent a dramatic facelift. The dome and the columned front entry were removed, and the entire structure was transformed into the Territorial style, a look that was more in step with Santa Fe architecture. After 1966, when the most recent state capitol was completed, the old structure continued to house a number of state offices. It was renamed the Bataan Memorial Building in honor of the New Mexicans who perished in or survived the 1942 Bataan Death March in World War II. The arched top-level windows are among the few still identifiable vestiges of the original exterior.

La Parroquia, circa 1867

The first church on this site was built in the 1620s and was destroyed during the Pueblo Revolt of 1680. It was replaced in the 1710s by the adobe Parroquia, or parish church, seen here, which served as Santa Fe's main church for more than a century and a half. The northern portion of the transept, at left in this photograph, is known as La Conquistadora Chapel. It was dedicated to a sixteenth-century wooden statue that was first brought to Santa Fe in 1625 and was later credited for helping in the eventual Spanish reconquest.

St. Francis of Assisi Cathedral

Archbishop Lamy ordered the construction of a cathedral—the first to be built west of the Mississippi River —in 1869 to replace the old Parroquia. St. Francis of Assisi Cathedral was built around the old adobe church (see p. 6), which was then dismantled, adobe brick by adobe brick. La Conquistadora Chapel, however, was preserved and incorporated into the cathedral, where it is still home to its namesake statue. The stone cathedral's French Romanesque design called for twin steeples rising to a height of a hundred and sixty feet, but they were never built owing to a lack of funds.

San Miguel Church, circa 1873

Santa Fe's San Miguel Church has endured, in various forms, for nearly four centuries. Franciscan missionaries constructed the original building, probably around the time of Santa Fe's founding in 1610, primarily to serve Mexican Indian servants living in the nearby Analco section of town, south of the Santa Fe River. The building was demolished in 1640, however, during a power struggle among Spanish officials. Although it was built anew, Indians burned it down during the 1680 Pueblo Revolt. San Miguel was rebuilt once again in 1710, and around 1830 the three-tiered tower was added, as shown in this well-known photograph by Timothy H. O'Sullivan.

Shortly after O'Sullivan photographed San Miguel Church, a windstorm blew down its tower, and the building remained in sad disrepair for more than a decade. In 1887, the church finally underwent a major restoration, including the addition of two masonry buttresses designed to strengthen the structure. In 1955, the tower was reworked into the form we see today. At that time, a thorough archaeological and historical analysis of the old church dated its physically traceable lineage back to 1710. Through the trees to the left is Santa Fe's so-called Oldest House, and on the right is the roofed balcony of the Lamy Building, formerly Saint Michael's College, built in 1878.

San Miguel Church Interior, circa 1873

Timothy H. O'Sullivan photographed the interior of San Miguel Church as well as the exterior. Much of the artwork here dates back to the seventeenth century and includes fine early examples of the craftsmanship of the santeros, painters and carvers of religious art. The beautiful, twenty-two-foot-tall hand-hewn altar screen, the gift of Antonio José Ortiz, was painted in 1798. Some of the paintings that adorn the walls were applied to tanned buffalo hide. I wonder if the man kneeling in the pew here is the same man that is standing in the doorway of O'Sullivan's outside view (opposite page), and if he was perhaps the priest.

During the restoration and archaeological analysis of San Miguel Church in the mid-1950s, conservators used a hundred gallons of solvent to strip away five time-hardened coats of house paint from the sanctuary's altar screen. Slowly, over a four-month period, the detailed 1798 handiwork by the screen's original artist, known as the Laguna Santero, emerged and was carefully restored. The church's old 780-pound bell, which rather mysteriously is adorned with the date "1356" (many feel this was an error and that instead it should read "1856"), now sits in the church's adjoining visitor center.

Santa Fe Plaza, circa 1855

This is one of the earliest known photographs of Santa Fe. It's also the oldest photograph in this book's "then" view of New Mexico. Central in this scene of the Plaza's southeastern corner is the Exchange Hotel, the capital's sole lodging establishment at the time. To the right is the Seligman and Clever mercantile company. Co-owner Siegmund Seligman was a German immigrant who probably came to town via the Santa Fe Trail, which ended here at the Plaza. Interestingly, he is also the earliest known New Mexico photographer, having operated a short-lived daguerreotype portrait studio prior to opening the business seen here. Seligman's business partner and fellow German immigrant, Charles Clever, later quit the partnership to become a lawyer and eventually served as a territorial delegate to Congress.

In response to the increasing importance of New Mexico's tourist trade, La Fonda Hotel was built in 1919 on the site of the old Exchange Hotel. Its construction was funded by the issuance of $200,000 in bonds, and investors were reportedly given rides in a World War I–era tank to assist with the demolition of the old hotel. The Plaza continues to be Santa Fe's business and cultural focal point, as it has been for nearly four hundred years. I photographed the scene on a quiet winter day.

Acequia Madre, circa 1915

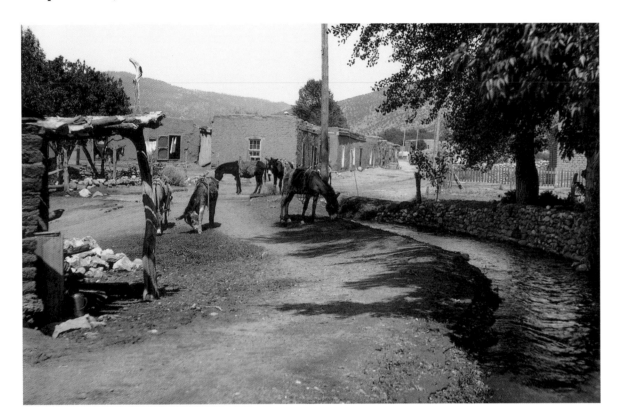

When the Spanish colonists came to New Mexico, they brought with them a knowledge and tradition of community irrigation systems. Santa Fe's Acequia Madre ("mother ditch") dates back to the town's origin. In fact, whenever a new community was settled, one of the first tasks undertaken by the townspeople was the construction of their irrigation system. Acequia Madre, which draws its water from the nearby Santa Fe River, is pictured here at its crossing with Canyon Road.

Acequias *play a vital role not only in the agricultural prosperity of Hispanic communities but also in the social and communal lives of the residents. Annual rites, such as the spring cleaning of a town's ditches, bring people together in efforts toward common goals. Acequia Madre is still used today—and its operation is still overseen by a* mayordomo, *or ditch boss. The neighborhood around this intersection of Canyon Road and Acequia Madre is one of Santa Fe's most desired—and expensive—residential areas, offering a taste of the charm and tradition of long ago for which the city is known. However, as seen here, SUVs are a much more common sight today than burros.*

View from Talaya Hill, circa 1935

T. Harmon Parkhurst shot this fine overview of eastern Santa Fe from the top of Talaya Hill, a low summit that stands a couple of miles west of Atalaya Mountain. Agricultural fields cover much of the valley bottom on the far side of the Santa Fe River, which flows down from the high country of the Sangre de Cristo Mountains, visible in the background. Santa Fe's population at this time was less than fifteen thousand, and only a handful of homes were located on this far eastern side of the town.

Santa Fe has experienced a fivefold increase in population since Parkhurst photographed this scene. The once rural landscape east of downtown is now dotted with homes, and the Sangre de Cristo foothills have proven to be a particularly desirable residential area. A few vestiges of the canyon-bottom fields remain, although little farming goes on today. The pronounced increase in tree cover has greatly altered this scene, and I had to move downslope a short distance from Parkhurst's hilltop vantage point to find an open view for my shot. Note that a water tank has replaced the large, open reservoir in the historical image.

UPPER RIO GRANDE

Taos Pueblo, 1941. Photograph by Ansel Adams.

"Land of Enchantment" has been New Mexico's slogan since 1934, but the enchantment itself has been sensed by New Mexican people for centuries. The locations of prehistoric pueblos, for example, reveal that their builders had an eye for dramatic settings at least a thousand years ago. Similarly, the journals of tough-minded Spanish explorers sometimes mention the sweep and grandeur of the land. So, too, in the years since territorial days, a stream of photographers, writers, and artists has been drawn to New Mexico by what they have called its magic and infectious charm. Many are those who have taken up camera, pen, or paintbrush to express that which can be felt as well as seen about New Mexico.

The variety of natural features and natural landscapes is a great part of the enchantment. In the north, the ranges of the Rocky Mountains reach from Colorado into New Mexico on either side of the Rio Grande, their snowy peaks, deep forests, and tumbling streams providing backdrops for Hispanic towns and villages nestled in the foothills.

The range on the eastern side is the Sangre de Cristo, with New Mexico's highest summits. Its very name, "blood of Christ," is laden with emotion, connoting both the sunset glow of the mountains and the faith of the villagers.

On the western side of the river stand the Tusas Mountains, a forest-and-meadow vastness reaching from the state line to the gorges of the Rio Chama. South of the gorges are the volcanic Jemez Mountains and their gigantic Valles Caldera. These mountains are a great jumble of hard rocks and soft rocks, of peaks and lofty, forested plateaus, of meadows and narrow canyons. Liberally studded with archaeological sites—pueblos and cliff dwellings—these mountains also mark the late stages of the long, prehistoric migration of Pueblo Indian ancestors from the Four Corners region to the Rio Grande.

Literally the "great river," the Rio Grande drains the mountains on both its sides as well as many in Colorado. The river flows for miles in a deep basaltic gorge, which finally widens into the Española Valley, where several villages divert the river's water for irrigation. Most communities of the area, however, take their water from the smaller mountain streams that flow down to join the Rio Grande. But the Rio Grande remains the fluid spine and lifeblood of all this part of New Mexico. Early in colonial times the area became known as the *Rio Arriba*, or Upper Rio Grande.

≈ ≈ ≈ ≈

When the first photographers arrived in Santa Fe, the Rio Arriba had been inhabited by the Pueblo Indians for many centuries, and then by the Hispanic people from 1598. The history was all quite shadowy, but the photographers immediately found the people interesting and certainly different, and they were eager to picture both groups—both the Indians and the Hispanic "natives." The Pueblo people were especially accessible, even to those who used the most bulky camera equipment, for they lived in unique, multi-storied adobe villages, some of them just up the road from Santa Fe. Many Pueblo individuals were also on good terms with Hispanic neighbors. Among the photographers who worked here were Timothy H. O'Sullivan, John Hillers, and Ben Wittick and, somewhat later, Charles Lummis and T. Harmon Parkhurst.

The Hispanic people of the Rio Arriba were equally alluring. Their forbears had come with the conquerors, and they were now the citizens of Santa Fe, Santa Cruz, Taos, and a host of other villages and communities scattered through the mountain valleys and down the length of the Rio Grande. Most of the Hispanic settlements of New Mexico were in the Rio Arriba, though others dotted the lower Rio Grande, the eastern plains out along the Santa Fe Trail, and the broad valleys of the Pecos, Canadian, and Mimbres Rivers.

Apparently some of the studio photographers in Santa Fe traveled by horse and wagon to make portraits and family pictures in smaller Hispanic communities. A number of them made panoramas of the villages, as well as pictures of individual houses, plazas, and churches, and of such subjects as religious processions, farmers in the fields, and livestock being driven around and around the threshing floors.

This was the stuff of folklore, of a history and of ways of life largely unknown to people in the rest of the United States. The villages were unique: striking adobe dwellings, some clustered around dusty plazas, and some strung along *acequias*, the ditches that brought water from the streams to the fields. There was also a singular look to the setting of these places: mountain backdrops, piñon-studded hills, dry arroyos. Nothing here looked like the towns or farmsteads of the Eastern states.

Even more distinctive were things that cameras could not record, such as tightly knit families and communities, and a Spanish dialect that was archaic from long isolation. In Hispanic communities, people worked together to mud-plaster their homes and churches, to maintain the *acequias*, to graze their sheep, and to celebrate the holy days and festivals of the Catholic faith.

Dye Lumber Company, 1908. Sawmill and lumber camp at Pines in upper Cochití Canyon, Jemez Mountains.

John Dunn Bridge, circa 1900. Spanning the Rio Grande near the confluence of the Rio Hondo and replacing two earlier bridges washed out by flooding, this toll bridge was the keystone of the roadside-hotel and transport business near Taos owned by colorful entrepreneur Dunn.

Nowhere else had the westward expansion of the United States encountered another European-derived society occupying an area of its own. Despite the long isolation of the New Mexico people, clearly their Spanish culture had been impressed upon the land for centuries. Hispanic and Indian peoples represented an overwhelming majority in the remote new Territory, while the Anglos (including virtually all the photographers for quite some years) were a definite minority.

Furthermore, while the annexation of New Mexico by the United States meant that Anglo-American government and institutions became the order of the day, the Hispanic people were accorded political and social equality from the first. What wisdom it was that the Hispanic heritage of New Mexico was viewed, both then and now, in a positive light. Or, as it could be said, today's multiculturalism began early in New Mexico.

≈   ≈   ≈   ≈

During the 1800s the town of Taos became a trade center for the upper Rio Grande, though even today the town retains the feel of a village. Good farmland and pasture around Taos led to the prosperity of several landowners. Kit Carson and his Hispanic wife lived in a rambling adobe near the plaza, and several other old-time trappers and mountain men gave Taos a rough cosmopolitan character.

Then early in the 1900s, Taos was also discovered by artists—painters, writers, photographers—and their patrons. A 1910 view of the town plaza, shown on page 40, hints of currents of old and new.

Soon, influenced by the newcomer artists of both Taos and Santa Fe, New Mexico's reputation for quaintness and picturesqueness grew, and in time a few Hispanic villages of the Sangre de Cristos came to be recognized as particularly charming. One of them was Las Trampas (The Traps). Here the church stands as the very model of a village church, made perfect in the early days by miniature wooden towers, or cupolas, atop its adobe façade. But the cupolas crumbled away and were forgotten for several decades, until in 1967 the community became the focus of a battle for historic preservation. The battle was successfully won when insensitive highway improvements through the heart of the village were forestalled; at the same time, the church was restored and the original towers re-created. The design of the replicas, and even knowledge of the existence of the original cupolas, depended on historical photographs such as the one by Jesse Nusbaum on page 36.

Meanwhile at Chimayó, another mountain village, there was, and is, a chapel known for its healing earth. The chapel, or *santuario*, was a gem of eighteenth-century architecture and religious art, quite apart from the soil that can still be scooped from a small hole in the floor of a sacristy room. Nusbaum's 1912 photos of the chapel have the look of age, as do Bill Stone's new photos, although the use of color film lends a different perception (see pp. 30, 31).

≈   ≈   ≈   ≈

At the same time that the early photographers were recording what they felt to be picturesque about the Rio Arriba, others things were happening to "develop" New Mexico. Most important were the construction of railroads and, especially in the Rio Arriba, timber cutting and sawmill operations. The historical photos here show glimpses of the sawmills at El Vado (p. 23) and Cochití Canyon (opposite page), as well as the pre-sawn railroad ties that were floated down Embudo Creek (p. 34).

A steel span slightly downriver replaced Dunn's wooden bridge years ago. On the far shore, the old road is mostly overgrown. Robust riverside vegetation reflects today's less-variable, dam-controlled flow. This is the put-in for rafters taking on the famous Taos Box stretch of the Rio Grande.

As rough and steep as the Rio Grande Gorge and the entire Rio Arriba are, completing even a single railroad in the area would have seemed unlikely. Yet in the late 1800s and early 1900s, railroads were surveyed and built across many remote locations. The Denver & Rio Grande Railroad (D&RG) built two rail lines in northern New Mexico. One was a line from Colorado to Santa Fe that slanted steeply down the Rio Grande Gorge. A part of this line is shown in William Henry Jackson's photograph on page 32.

The second line of the D&RG would become one of the most spectacular narrow-gauge mountain railroads in the West. As shown in a Jackson photo on page 22, this line departed from the D&RG's standard-gauge line at Antonito, Colorado, to wind through canyons, gorges, and high passes along the Colorado–New Mexico boundary on its way to both Farmington, New Mexico, and Silverton, Colorado.

Except for tourist excursion runs on the old narrow-gauge, now called the Cumbres & Toltec Scenic Railroad, neither of these rail lines still exists. New Mexico's Upper Rio Grande remains the state's historic heart, but evidently it no longer needs a railroad.

Mesa Montosa Cliffs, 1917

The striking cliffs along the western edge of Mesa Montosa, near the confluence of Canjilon Creek and the Rio Chama, caught the eye of geologist N. H. Darton. During a visit in 1917, he made several photographs of this colorful escarpment, including this fine view. Darton's primary photographic interest here was probably in documenting the five distinct geologic strata that are exposed in the cliffs. These formations were laid down during the Mesozoic Era, some two hundred fifty to sixty-five million years ago. Three-quarters of the world's existing plant and animal species became extinct near the end of this time period.

In 1947, paleontologist Edwin Colbert found the complete fossilized skeletons of hundreds of Coelophysis—a larger-than-man-sized carnivorous dinosaur that walked on two legs—at the base of these cliffs, just off the right edge of this scene. Paleontologists believe that these dinosaurs died of thirst at a depleted water source. The water finally returned, but as a flash flood that buried them until they were uncovered millions of years later. Today, Coelophysis, also sometimes known as Rioarribasaurus, is New Mexico's state fossil. Artist Georgia O'Keeffe loved this area. In 1937, she began renting and later bought from Ghost Ranch's Arthur Pack a small house, Rancho de los Burros, tucked up against the base of these cliffs. There she lived seasonally for several years before moving full-time to nearby Abiquiu following the death of her husband, photographer Alfred Stieglitz.

Toltec Tunnel, Toltec Gorge, circa 1880

Starting from Alamosa, Colorado, the Denver & Rio Grande Railroad began construction westward on its narrow-gauge San Juan extension in early 1880. The first train arrived in the new town of Chama, New Mexico, on the last day of the same year. However, the first formal excursion on the line was made in October, with famed western photographer William Henry Jackson aboard. A literary cadre of Colorado newspaper editors and their wives also went along and decided that the name "Toltec" should be used for both the tunnel and the deep, rugged gorge nearby. Jackson's photograph of the train's passengers posed at the west portal of the Toltec Tunnel may document this October 4–5, 1880, inaugural trip along the extension route. Jackson also climbed to the top of the ridge above the tunnel to photograph Toltec Gorge, looking west. The Rio de los Pinos flows within the sheer-walled depths of the gorge.

It was a hundred and twenty-two years, to the day, after the inaugural train passed through the Toltec Tunnel—and thirty-two years, to the day, after the first tourist train made the trip—that I hiked the three miles along the rails from Osier, Colorado, to the tunnel to make my photographs. I opted to photograph the tunnel scene with the Cumbres & Toltec Scenic Railroad train, now jointly operated by New Mexico and Colorado, entering the sunlit west portal on its way back to Antonito, Colorado. The train crew had waved enthusiastically when they saw me. In the gorge scene, I caught the C&TS train just after it had exited the tunnel. Colorful fall aspens highlight the area where a forest fire burned a large stand of evergreens in 1879. The Garfield Monument, visible just beyond the tunnel's west portal, was erected on this spot in honor of President James A. Garfield, who was slain in 1881.

Imagine this scene with the slopes covered by forests of beautiful ponderosa pines, many four feet in diameter and a hundred and fifty feet tall. That's the picture that encouraged the New Mexico Lumber Company, in 1903, to establish the sawmill and logging camp called El Vado (The Crossing), referring to the nearby, easily forded stretch of the Rio Chama. The Rio Grande & Southwestern narrow-gauge railroad provided the means both to transport the cut timber to El Vado for milling and to export the processed lumber to market.

By 1923, loggers had harvested all of the El Vado area's accessible timber. The New Mexico Lumber Company dismantled the entire facility and moved it to Colorado, and the rails followed shortly thereafter. In the early 1930s, El Vado Dam was built across a narrowing of the Rio Chama a short distance downriver from the site of the logging camp. I photographed this scene, including drought-diminished El Vado Lake and the dam—both now within El Vado Lake State Park—from a lake-bisecting ridge called the Peninsula. Notice the building foundation on the beach and the contoured shoreline terraces, both exposed as the lake level receded.

Soda Dam, circa 1885

A mile up the Jemez River from the site of Guisewa Pueblo, calcium-carbonate-laden hot mineral water, a legacy of the area's volcanic origin, has formed a travertine ridge—the Soda Dam. Creating a natural barrier across the canyon, the dam has been penetrated by the river's flow, which, judging by the accumulated debris seen here, can at times be considerable. High up on the canyon's west wall, out of the view shown here, are the remains of older natural dams that were formed before the river cut down to its present level.

The Soda Dam has been attracting visitors through the years. The Ancestral Puebloan people who lived near here most certainly were curious about it. Today it's not uncommon in the warmer months to find kids of all ages here climbing over the rocks, jumping into the pools, and sliding down the water chutes. Close comparison of these images reveals that some details of the dam have changed, while others have persisted. I asked my wife, Carolyn, to strike a pose similar to that of one of the men in Ben Wittick's old photograph.

Mission Church at Guisewa Pueblo, 1880

Jemez State Monument

Ancestors of today's Jemez Indians built Guisewa Pueblo around 1300 in a small side canyon just off the Jemez River. At its height in population, the three-story village was home to as many as eight hundred people. In the early 1600s, Spanish colonizers built a mission church here, but Navajo raids soon led to the abandonment of the pueblo and the destruction of the church. By 1627, the church had been rebuilt and the pueblo reoccupied, but most habitation at the site ended during the Pueblo Revolt. John Hillers photographed the massive ruins of the sandstone-and-adobe church and convento *(priests' quarters) in 1880. The flat-roofed building and corral structures were "site improvements" made by a local sheepherding squatter who settled right in amidst the ruins.*

Archaeological surveys of Guisewa Pueblo and its mission church in the 1920s and '30s led to some interesting findings. A series of colorful frescoes was found adorning the walls of the church nave. Church builders had also used several panes of selenite, a variety of translucent gypsum, for windows. Today the ruins comprise Jemez State Monument, and the squatter's building has been removed. The hillside behind the church has more piñon and juniper trees on its slopes today than it did in Hillers' day. I was barely able to get this clear shot through the dense stand of trees that now covers the ridge just south of the site. I was probably within twenty-five feet of the original camera location.

Chama River, 1889

Shot from high ground along the east side of the Chama River, this photograph includes the river canyon with just a trace of water, Cañones Creek flowing toward the camera and into the Chama along the left edge, and prominent Pedernal Peak of the northern Jemez Mountains in the background. The confluence of the Chama and Cañones was the general locale of several late-nineteenth-century placer mining claims, including those called the Daniel Boone, the Brandenburg, and the Sally Heston. The large, bowl-like depression in the right half of the scene is a small part of the Piedra Lumbre basin, a name derived from El Valle de Piedra Lumbre, or The Valley of Shining Stone.

Abiquiu Lake

In 1962, the federal government completed construction of Abiquiu Dam, just off the left edge of this view. The subsequent flooding of portions of the Piedra Lumbre changed the basin forever and caused great pain for many of the area's longtime residents. Much of the water impounded in Abiquiu Lake originates in tributaries of the San Juan River, on the opposite side of the Continental Divide, and is brought across via the divide-spanning, thirteen-mile-long Azotea Tunnel. This infrastructure is part of the San Juan–Chama Project, which will annually provide, via the Rio Grande, nearly 50,000 acre-feet of water to Albuquerque. The city has been paying for this project since the 1960s, and is now developing the ability to harvest the flow, possibly by utilizing an inflatable dam on the Rio Grande in Albuquerque's North Valley.

Ceremonial Cave at Frijoles Canyon, circa 1912

Alcove House, Bandelier National Monument

Jesse Nusbaum photographed San Ildefonso artist Julían Martínez as he posed on the kiva ladder in the Ceremonial Cave, a natural alcove a hundred and fifty feet up the east wall of Frijoles Canyon. The kiva had been excavated just a few years earlier in 1908, and archaeologists had found nearly perfectly preserved matting, red corn, and other artifacts left by the Ancestral Puebloan people who lived here in prehistoric time. The kiva's upper walls and roof were reconstructed by Nusbaum in 1910. Martínez was the husband of María Martínez, perhaps the most famous of all Pueblo potters. Together, the Martínezes rediscovered and perfected the techniques for making the highly prized San Ildefonso black-on-black pottery.

Bandelier National Monument was established in 1916. Park officials recently changed the name of Ceremonial Cave to Alcove House because they felt the original name was misleading: The site had been primarily residential, not ceremonial. The holes and openings in the back wall are remnants from the cluster of twenty-two masonry-walled rooms that were incorporated into the alcove's natural architecture. The low winter sun allowed me just a few minutes of light on the kiva for my shot before sinking below the mesa across the canyon. I enlisted a couple visiting from San Francisco to replicate the people in Nusbaum's shot, and politely requested that the dozen or so other site-swarming visitors step aside momentarily while I made my exposures. The pine trees along the far rim of Frijoles Canyon burned during a 1974 forest fire.

Santa Cruz Church, 1880s

During the Spanish reconquest and resettlement of New Mexico following the Pueblo Revolt of 1680, Diego de Vargas founded in 1695 New Mexico's second oldest municipality, La Villa Nueva de Santa Cruz de la Cañada. For a few years, Santa Cruz's new residents worshipped in a chapel that had been built by the Indians. Then in 1733, construction was started on a new church, Santa Cruz de la Cañada, which was completed ten years later. Artists decorated and furnished the adobe and mud structure's interior with beautiful santero art, much of which has survived to the present. William Henry Jackson made this image of the church during one of his trips through northern New Mexico.

I photographed the Santa Cruz Church on a beautiful fall Sunday morning while Mass was being celebrated. Moments after I tripped the shutter, the church doors opened and dozens of parishioners streamed out and headed off to after-church dinner. By the time I could pack up my camera gear, the parking lot was all but empty. Around 1900, the church's roof was changed from its leak-prone flat design to a pitched profile sheathed with iron. The bell tower collapsed in 1999 and was rebuilt just two years before I photographed the church. In spite of the many updates that have taken place over the years, many of the building's architectural features have survived.

Santuario de Chimayó, 1911

Built in the 1810s by Don Bernardo Abeyta as a private chapel, the Santuario de Chimayó occupies a classic northern New Mexico setting, near the village of Chimayó, a place known for its talented weavers. Many believe that this little church was built on sacred earth that possesses miraculous healing ability. Since the church's early days, believers in this power have come here to be cured of a variety of infirmities. A small pit in the floor of a corner room contains the healing earth that pilgrims take with them when they leave.

The Santuario was passed down through the Abeyta family for many generations until 1929, when it was purchased by a group of Santa Fe residents, including architect John Gaw Meem, who eventually turned it over to the Archdiocese of Santa Fe. The pitched roof, seen here, was added in the 1920s, and other cosmetic changes have been made over the years. The church is still the destination of cure-seeking pilgrims, and thousands of faithful participate in the annual Holy Week pilgrimage to the shrine, which was added to the National Register of Historic Places in 1970.

Santuario de Chimayó Interior, 1911

When Don Bernardo Abeyta built his chapel, he also commissioned several santeros to paint the ornate wooden retablos (altar screens) and to carve the bultos (statues) that adorn the sanctuary. The scenes depicted on this artwork portray a number of figures and events of importance to Catholics. The rustic simplicity of the chapel is typical of northern New Mexico's traditional style.

The Santuario's unique collection of Spanish Colonial religious art has endured for nearly two centuries. Curious visitors and pilgrims alike still admire this work of the talented artists of the 1800s. A door just to the left of the altar leads to the small room containing the pit filled with the sacred earth. The adjoining sacristy is filled with devotional objects, including crutches of the once-infirmed faithful who attribute their healing to the curative power found here. The nave today is filled with pews for those attending Mass or wishing to pray for a while in this venerated place.

Rio Grande near Embudo, circa 1900

After failing to secure the rights to enter New Mexico from Colorado via Raton Pass, owners of the Denver & Rio Grande Railroad decided to run the line southward from Alamosa, along the west side of the Rio Grande, to Santa Fe. The Chili Line, as this Santa Fe branch was known, opened for traffic to Española on the last day of 1880. Later, William Henry Jackson photographed this fine view of the Rio Grande Valley near Embudo, with the rails of the Comanche Canyon section of the Chili Line in the foreground. With a four-percent grade and sharp curves, the ride down Comanche Canyon to the Rio Grande at Embudo Station must have been exciting.

The Chili Line was abandoned in 1941, and the rails were removed the following year. The rail bed in the scene is now part of a private driveway, and the property owner kindly gave me permission to scout the scene and make my photograph. The hillside road on the right of Jackson's image has completely eroded away, and the river today is hidden by shoreline cottonwood growth. Considerably more people now inhabit and farm the valley lowlands of the central area of the scene than in Chili Line days.

Embudo Creek, circa 1915

Vermonter A. B. McGaffey formed the Santa Barbara Pole and Tie Company in 1907 to meet the Santa Fe Railway's healthy demand for ties. Timber was harvested on the slopes of the Santa Barbara Grant and cut into ties at a sawmill at nearby Hodges. The ties were then floated down Embudo Creek, seen here, to its confluence with the Rio Grande, where they were held until early summer. With adequate flow in the Rio Grande, the logjam was released and the ties—four hundred thousand in a typical year—floated through White Rock Canyon to a place near Cochití Pueblo named Boom, where they were pulled from the river and loaded onto railcars for shipment to Albuquerque.

Ties are no longer floated down Embudo Creek, and, given the rather minimal late-autumn flow that I photographed, it's hard to imagine that many would even be able to make it the two miles through to the Rio Grande. Over the years, the main creek channel has narrowed and the cottonwoods have proliferated. I had to climb up the steep creek bank a bit from where the old shot was taken to get an open view for my photograph. An elderly resident of Dixon, who lives just out of this scene to the right, recounted to me that his father used to talk about the ties that were penned up on the Embudo, waiting for the adequate flow that would carry them downriver. He said that sometimes they would be loaded onto wagons and transported instead by an overland route.

Las Trampas, 1912

The village of Las Trampas was established in the mid-1700s by a dozen families from Santa Fe. An agricultural community, early-day Las Trampas served somewhat as a buffer between the settlements along the Rio Grande and the Apache and Ute Indians. The village at one time had a defensive adobe wall surrounding the central plaza area to help protect its residents. The prominent San José de Gracia Church, completed in 1776, stands near the center of this Jesse Nusbaum photograph, with the schoolhouse just to the left of the church.

In spite of some readily apparent differences between these two photographs, much of Las Trampas looks the same today as it did almost a century ago. The church was extensively restored in the 1980s, and it is considered to be the best-preserved Spanish Colonial church in the country. In the 1960s, a group of preservationists banded together to prevent the highway department from paving the road past the churchyard. The plaza is still the heart of the town, although the defensive wall is gone.

The first mission churches at Picurís Pueblo occupied sites that were somewhat removed from the main pueblo. In 1769, raiding Comanches sacked the outlying church, and the governor of New Mexico ordered a replacement to be built adjacent to the pueblo. Much of the lumber, including doors and balustrades, was salvaged from the razed church and recycled. The new church, which is the structure seen in this photograph, was in use by 1776, the year Father Domínguez visited Picurís.

Like many of the adobe buildings in the Southwest, the church at Picurís Pueblo has been renovated several times over the years. For several decades in the twentieth century, it sported a pitched metal roof. In the 1960s, it was almost completely rebuilt, with a reversion to the old Mission style. Another overhaul in the 1990s resulted in the church as we see it here, and many volunteers from the area around Picurís helped apply the traditional mud plaster finish coat. Today, the population of Picurís Pueblo is just a few hundred —a far cry from the days when it was one of the largest Tiwa pueblos.

Church Ruins and Cemetery, Taos Pueblo, circa 1880s

Taos Pueblo, the northernmost of the Rio Grande pueblos, occupies a scenic setting along the Rio Pueblo de Taos at the foot of the Sangre de Cristo Mountains. Following the arrival of the Spaniards, the first mission church, San Geronimo de Taos, was built in 1627 and destroyed in an uprising twelve years later. The church was rebuilt but again met a similar fate, along with all other visible symbols of Spanish rule, during the 1680 Pueblo Revolt. Following the reconquest by the Spaniards, yet another mission —built with thick walls of adobe and adorned with a bell tower, pictured here—was constructed. This church was so substantial that it adequately doubled as a fortress against a Comanche attack in 1776.

In spite of the structural strength of the Taos church, it was unable to withstand a bombardment inflicted on it by U.S. troops and militiamen during an 1847 attack. The American forces were in pursuit of Hispanic rebels and Taos Indians, who took refuge inside the building after killing territorial Governor Charles Bent and other local officials, in protest of the newly emplaced American governance. The rebel revolt was quickly suppressed, and many of the participants who weren't killed during the conflict were later hanged for treason. The church was nearly demolished during the attack and has been preserved in that state as a memorial to those who were killed. The cemetery around the church ruins is still used by the pueblo.

Taos Plaza, circa 1910

Taos was settled in the 1700s by Spanish colonists who had been farming the land around nearby Taos Pueblo. During New Mexico's quarter-century under Mexican rule, Taos became known as a trading center, and by the early twentieth century, it had developed a reputation for cultural heritage and natural beauty. This view of the busy plaza was shot during the era when the automobile was replacing the horse-drawn wagon. By this time, most of the earlier plaza's private homes had been replaced by businesses.

During the first decades of the twentieth century, Taos evolved into a thriving artists' colony, a trend that has continued to this day. Numerous art galleries attract art collectors and viewers from near and far, and many accomplished artists still live and work in the area. The plaza continues as the town's focal point, although the early morning activity I encountered when I made this photograph from atop a shop portal was a far cry from what is seen in the 1910 view. I made my shot in the winter, with hopes that the bare-branch view would show more of the plaza than the full summer foliage would allow.

Red River, 1905

The town of Red River came to life as a mining camp in the 1890s with the discovery of gold in the area. By 1905, when this photograph was taken, a population of around three thousand bustled about the town that had grown quickly along the banks of the Red River. Gold was plentiful in surface deposits but petered out quickly with depth. It took just a few years for the more productive mines to be played out, and Red River's boom retreated almost as quickly as it came.

For several decades following the area's gold depletion, Red River slumbered. In the 1950s a few of the remaining residents decided that the town's real resource might just be its scenic location and the visitor amenities it could provide to vacationers. A ski area was built and started operation in 1959. Restaurants, accommodations, and stores soon followed. Red River has since been one of New Mexico's most popular mountain vacation towns. It's an important jumping-off place for those venturing into the backcountry of the surrounding Carson National Forest.

Northern New Mexico's Sangre de Cristo Mountains feature some of the state's most beautiful and pristine high-mountain country. Forests of spruce, fir, and pine are accented by aspen groves that turn gloriously colorful in autumn. In 1887, one of the largest forest fires in the area's recorded history started burning in Big Tesuque Canyon. For two months, the blaze consumed trees and ground cover as it burned across the slopes of Lake Peak, Santa Fe Baldy, and Pecos Baldy and eventually jumped the Pecos River. Crews cutting timber for railroad ties were finally able to contain it. T. Harmon Parkhurst's photo, shot thirty-some years after the fire, records the destruction left behind by this conflagration.

These photographs were made from an elevation of 12,400 feet on the summit of Lake Peak, a short distance north of today's Ski Santa Fe resort. The view looks down on Puerto Nambé in the center, across to Santa Fe Baldy on the left, and beyond to the Truchas Peaks in the far background, a dozen miles to the northeast—all within the Santa Fe National Forest's Pecos Wilderness. My photograph, made eighty years after Parkhurst's, documents the slow recovery process that follows such a devastating fire.

Truchas, circa 1935

The village of Truchas is a classic northern New Mexico town of Hispanic origin. With a backdrop of the beautiful Truchas Peaks, seen here, Truchas dates back to the eighteenth century. In 1770, the isolated village reportedly had more than a hundred residents, an impressive population for the time and place. This roadside descanso, *or shrine, greeted people as they entered the town from the west.*

Today's motorists driving the scenic High Road to Taos still see a descanso *as they enter Truchas, in the same spot as the one pictured seventy years ago. This rough-hewn cross is less ornate than the old one, and its new concrete base is perhaps less aesthetically appealing than the pile of rocks, but the symbolic meaning is still the same. Even the nearby outbuilding is ecclesiastically adorned! Truchas hasn't changed dramatically since T. Harmon Parkhurst photographed the village, although it is now popular with tourists wanting to sample old northern New Mexico. The filming here in 1988 of the Robert Redford movie based on John Nichols'* The Milagro Beanfield War *has inspired many visitors to come see the place.*

ALBUQUERQUE AND VICINITY

Hodgin Hall, University of New Mexico, 1905

≈ ≈ ≈ ≈

Albuquerque is New Mexico's largest city, though by Census Bureau standards it is only "mid-sized." In population rankings, the four hundred and fifty thousand people within the city limits make Albuquerque—surprisingly—the thirty-fifth largest of all the nation's cities. However, if the Bureau's more meaningful Metropolitan Statistical Areas (MSA) are compared, the seven hundred and thirty thousand people of the Albuquerque MSA (comprising Bernalillo, Sandoval, and Valencia Counties) yield a rank of seventy-third largest. Either way, Albuquerque's showing is remarkable for a community that had only about nine thousand people in 1890, around the time when several of this book's historical photographs were made.

Today's Albuquerque combines the look and feel of a modern city with quite a few remnants of the original Spanish Colonial settlement along the Rio Grande. Old Town is a vestige of the plaza-centered village founded in 1706, while downtown and its surrounding neighborhoods represent the new Albuquerque that came into being after the transcontinental railroad arrived in 1880. All the rest of the city, extending outward for miles in all directions, is the product of the twentieth century and the start of the twenty-first.

The railroad—the Atchison, Topeka & Santa Fe Railway, known as the Santa Fe—actually bypassed Old Town Albuquerque by a mile and a half, owing in part to the machinations of Anglo land speculators. In the open spaces between the old town and the railroad, they reckoned, money was to be made by the construction of a new American-style community of straight streets, city blocks, and neatly laid-out building lots for homes and businesses. Thus the new Albuquerque took on a character very different from that of the always plaza-oriented Santa Fe.

This new Albuquerque long since swallowed the old, and both are now surrounded by a solidly built-up urban area of more than a hundred and ten square miles, with another sizable undeveloped area within the city limits. Instrumental in this expansion have been today's counterparts of the original developers. In recent years, entrepreneurial builders have produced almost another new Albuquerque in the northwestern fringe of the city, not to mention an all-new adjoining city, Rio Rancho, just over the county line.

Some of the photographers who rode the train to Albuquerque in the 1880s stayed to open portrait studios and do "general" photography around town. First among them was Ben Wittick, who actually arrived a couple of years before the railroad did. Some of his photographs from 1881 are the earliest known pictures of new Albuquerque. Showing a portion of First Street, the photo on page 50 wonderfully portrays a raw, sun-washed but hopeful frontier town.

More important in the long run to recording the town was William Henry Cobb. With his wife, Eddie Ross Cobb, daughter of the territorial governor, Cobb made pictures in Albuquerque and Santa Fe during the 1890s and throughout the first decade of the 1900s. After his death in 1909, Mrs. Cobb carried on the work of the studio for many years. Their advertising card stated "Outside Views and Groups a Specialty," and indeed the Cobbs pictured many buildings and events that would otherwise be unknown today.

For a time, the photographers in Albuquerque seem to have divided their efforts between new Albuquerque and Old Town, and a favorite subject in Old Town was the historic church of San Felipe. The photo of the church that appears on page 48 was taken by William Henry Jackson, in 1890 or thereabout. As usual, Jackson made an effort to shoot from a good vantage point, this time a rooftop on the opposite side of the old plaza.

Then as the twentieth century got under way, new Albuquerque apparently became large enough and busy enough to capture most of the photographic attention. Our photo from 1905 (p. 52), for instance, shows an amazingly matured Second Street—substantial buildings as far as the eye can see, numerous wagons and buggies, and at least one electric streetlight.

But no automobiles yet appear. Records show only that by 1908 some thirty automobiles shared Albuquerque's streets with horses and wagons, and that the automobiles were known by some as devil wagons. In that year, which was also the occasion of another visit by photographer Jackson, the town council passed its first ordinance regulating the speed of motor vehicles.

Other photographers were also busy in those times, often recording social events, parades, and politicians. The *Albuquerque Daily Citizen* occasionally reported that one or another photographer had made "splendid pictures" at this or that event, though none of the pictures were ever published in the paper. For a small-town paper, that was a technical impossibility.

A number of old photos from the vicinity of Albuquerque are also telling for their depictions of the rural character of the city's surroundings. The pictures included here range in age from 1867 to

Albuquerque Fire Department demonstration, 1921

nearly modern times: the old church at Isleta Pueblo in a decrepit state (see p. 54), a survey being made for a never-to-be-constructed railroad through Tijeras Canyon (p. 53), the original highway bridge over the Rio Grande at Bernalillo (p. 56). A photograph by William Henry Cobb (below) depicts sheep being herded at Coyote Canyon, a place that is now within the confines of Kirtland Air Force Base.

One of the more interesting photographs of the Albuquerque vicinity is the 1937 picture of the Santa Fe–Albuquerque highway (see p. 58) by modernist Edward Weston (1886–1958). At one level, this is a plain picture of an unremarkable scene, yet how it summons up a time gone by—the more so by the contrast of Bill Stone's color photo at dusk. Only a bit of skyline reveals both pictures to be of the same place.

Throughout the early 1900s, Albuquerque was growing to become the largest town in New Mexico. Yet it remained quite a small place, with no more than thirty-five thousand people as late as 1940. Thereafter, as a result of military activity at the old landing strip that became Kirtland Air Force Base, and partly too because of the development of nuclear weapons in New Mexico, the town grew rapidly. By 1950, its population had reached ninety-seven thousand, and in another ten years it had risen to two hundred and one thousand. As with other cities in the mountain and desert West, World War II was a tremendous turning point; only then did such cities become truly knitted into the fabric of modern America.

≈ ≈ ≈ ≈

Bill Stone has noted that though many old photos of Albuquerque scenes exist in archives, quite a few of them cannot now be rephotographed. Many buildings have vanished, but more to the point, the historical vantage points and subjects are blocked off by buildings, trees, and other things that weren't present in earlier times. Where once a photo could show the fledgling University of New Mexico, then a single building (opposite page, p. 47) sitting forlornly on the mesa at a distance from town, now the space between the two is completely built up. Where once a photo could be made *from* the university, showing Albuquerque's Sandia Mountains off to the east, now the entire ten-mile distance to the mountains is an ocean of homes, shopping centers, schools, and all the other accouterments of the city.

The pattern of Albuquerque's growth, most of which occurred in the age of the automobile, has been not at all what the urbanists of older times described for American and European cities. Here the central business district has not to any great extent expanded *outward* into surrounding neighborhoods; nor has its expansion *upward*, as high-rise buildings, been more than modest. Instead, the central core moved to the outskirts. It decentralized, as thousands of commercial and institutional buildings, along with many thousands of new homes, sprawled to grazing lands around the town. Now many urban centers and sub-centers—be they for commercial, educational, governmental, manufacturing, or entertainment purposes—are the scattered foci of greater Albuquerque, connected by many miles of arterial streets.

For Bill's photographic endeavors, all this meant that Old Town and downtown were nearly the only places where contrasts between "then" and "now" could be seen. All the newer growth is in areas where few really old photos had ever been made.

≈ ≈ ≈ ≈

One of the most striking environmental changes in Albuquerque—and indeed in many other places in New Mexico—is the presence of trees where formerly there were few or none. Rio Grande cottonwoods, especially, were hardly to be seen along the banks and floodplains of the Rio Grande in the late 1800s and early 1900s. Numerous old photographs, made in dozens of towns and locations along the Rio Grande and other streams, show a barrenness that is now hard to believe.

Presumably this sterility existed because riparian, or riverside, trees were continually downed for firewood and light construction. In a land where real timber was limited to distant mountains, apparently people helped themselves to whatever was closer at hand. After a while there was nothing left, except probably along stretches of the rivers that were farthest from the towns.

Gradually this changed as other fuels, electricity, and good lumber came into use. Gradually the cottonwood groves and thickets returned, and gradually the towns and countryside assumed greener appearances. Riverside areas near Old Town and Atrisco in Albuquerque were formerly bare, but by the 1930s and 1940s they again had cottonwoods in abundance. Many residents today have assumed that the Rio Grande's cottonwood *bosque*, as the river forest has come to be known, is composed of trees hundreds of years old. In fact, most of the trees are relatively young.

Coyote Canyon, 1891. The canyon drains the west side of the northern end of the Manzano Mountains. Farming, mining, ranching, and mineral springs attracted early settlers. A large flock of sheep gathers around a watering hole at Coyote Springs in this William Henry Cobb photograph.

Kirtland Air Force Base. In 1942, the U.S. government acquired the Coyote Canyon area for what would become Kirtland AFB, a center for the nation's new nuclear weapons program. The hills in the background were hollowed out as a secure warehouse for the world's most powerful bombs.

Albuquerque from the East, 1883

Albuquerque's population was around five thousand and growing when this scene was photographed from the sand hills east of town. Until just three years earlier, Albuquerque had been mostly confined to the plaza-centered Old Town, or Old Albuquerque, area. Then, in April 1880, the Atchison, Topeka & Santa Fe Railway arrived, and everything changed. The railroad entered the area along a route two miles east of Old Town, and that's where New Albuquerque came to life, just west of the tracks. Most of the development seen here occurred in the few short years between the arrival of the railroad and the making of this photograph. Along the distant horizon stands the line of volcanoes on the mesa west of the Rio Grande.

It is impossible to photograph an identical view today. However, I was able to come quite close by scrambling to the top of the graded embankment along the west side of I-25, just south of Central Avenue. I decided on this vantage point only after spending several hours, on several days, searching the area for a good spot. Albuquerque's population has grown a hundredfold in a hundred and twenty years, and development extends out in all directions from the original downtown area. The volcanoes can still be seen between the skyscrapers and beyond the new downtown courthouses.

East Mesa, circa 1895

This southeasterly view of the sand hills immediately east of Albuquerque shows Hodgin Hall on the early University of New Mexico campus, backdropped by the distant Manzano Mountains. This photograph was taken about fifteen years after the arrival of the railroad in Albuquerque, at a time when most businesses and residences were still confined to the New Albuquerque and Old Town areas. To get up the hill to the campus from downtown New Albuquerque, students either walked or rode in a university-owned, four-horse hack.

When I found the old photograph of this view in the Albuquerque Museum's collection, I knew that I wanted to include it in this book. I also knew that reshooting this scene would be a challenge. After coming up empty-handed in my quest for a vantage point immediately west of campus, I decided to look farther away, near I-25. Following a thorough search, I realized that the only way to get my shot was to request permission, which was kindly granted, to shoot from a top-floor balcony of the eleven-story Encino Terrace, a senior retirement complex. To say that Albuquerque and the University of New Mexico have grown considerably in the past century would be an understatement.

Old Town, circa 1890

This fine William Henry Jackson photograph of Albuquerque's Old Town includes the picket fence–enclosed plaza with its corner turnstiles; the church of San Felipe de Neri, built in 1793 to replace its dilapidated predecessor on the plaza's west side; and several shops and residences. The one-hundred-and-twenty-foot-tall flagpole, reportedly the tallest west of the Mississippi River, was built in the 1860s by the U.S. Army. Many of the plaza's trees appear to be newly planted in this scene, which is backdropped by Albuquerque's volcanoes—seen here as small bumps along the distant horizon.

My efforts at replicating Jackson's photo of Old Town Albuquerque were frustrated by the view-blocking trees. I knew that I would be able to see more of the plaza if I waited until the trees were bare of their leaves. Therefore, I decided to try my shot when the plaza is in all its winter glory—on Christmas Eve. With permission from a shop owner, I climbed to the roof and positioned myself as close as possible to Jackson's camera location. As the sun set, I watched as volunteers scurried about to light the luminarias—the traditional Christmas decorations of sand-filled paper bags glowing with candles. I then waited for the optimal exposure balance between the waning skylight and the luminarias. The twin steeples of the church can barely be seen through the trees, and the volcanoes are now completely hidden.

First Street and Railroad Avenue, 1881

First Street and Central Avenue

The corner of First Street and Railroad Avenue is pictured here in July 1881, a little over a year after the first train arrived in Albuquerque. Hope's European Hotel and Restaurant occupies the corner building, a prefabricated structure that was hauled in by train— along the tracks lying a few hundred feet out of the picture to the left. The mule-drawn trolley, which provided service between New Albuquerque and Old Town, operated from 1881 to 1904.

Several street names were changed as Albuquerque grew, and for many decades this location has been the intersection of First Street and Central Avenue. All of the old buildings are long gone, but the trains still run along the tracks just out of the scene. In the last few years, major downtown renewal activity has changed the face of much of the city-center area. The entire complex seen here, including the multiplex theater and parking garage, was completed and opened for business while I worked on this project.

Ballooning, 1882

Albuquerque International Balloon Fiesta

On July 4, 1882, an Albuquerque saloonkeeper named Park Van Tassel filled a balloon with coal gas from the local gas works and made Albuquerque's first recorded balloon ascension. Residents had to forgo using their gas-fueled lights for two days so that enough gas could be stockpiled to fill the balloon, seen here about to be launched from a downtown site. "Professor" Van Tassel, as he was called following the historic flight, reportedly achieved an altitude exceeding 14,000 feet and landed in a cornfield near Old Town. He and his balloon then went on tour, and both apparently met their demise in the waters off Hawaii.

From a humble beginning in 1882, Albuquerque's involvement in ballooning has grown steadily through the years. Now known as the balloon capital of the world, the Albuquerque area attracts balloonists because of its favorable terrain and wind patterns. In 1972, thirteen hot-air balloons participated in the first gathering of what is now called the Albuquerque International Balloon Fiesta. With nearly a thousand balloons flying and a million spectators watching, the fiesta is the largest such event in the world today. The colorful mass ascension, seen here, in which hundreds of balloons lift off together, is always a crowd-pleaser.

Second Street and Silver Avenue, 1905

Looking north along Second Street from the corner of Silver Avenue, this view of New Albuquerque shows how quickly the new downtown area grew after the arrival of the railroad. Just fifteen years earlier, when the train chugged into town for the first time, there was very little here. At the time of this photograph, however, Albuquerque had a population of well over ten thousand and was starting to look like a sizable town. New Albuquerque's post office was established in 1881, occupying two Gold Avenue locations before moving here. Note the electric street light suspended above the intersection, the fire hydrant on the left, and the bicycles.

Sadly, urban-renewal projects undertaken over the years have removed virtually all of the buildings seen in the accompanying historical view. The scene today is dominated by Albuquerque's downtown skyscrapers, La Posada Hotel, and a new city-owned, multi-level parking structure. Today's downtown business center has shifted location a few blocks to the north and west from what it was a century ago. One thing hasn't changed—the fire hydrant on the left is in about the same place as the one seen in the old picture.

Tijeras Canyon, 1867

The gap between the Sandia and Manzano Mountains east of Albuquerque, Tijeras Canyon has long been an important travel corridor linking the Rio Grande Valley with the Estancia Basin. Paleo-Indians of more than a millennium ago, Spanish settlers of a few centuries ago, and immigrants and armies of the nineteenth century all followed a dusty trail through the canyon that, over time, evolved into a rough wagon road. In 1867, the Kansas-Pacific Railroad Company surveyed Tijeras Canyon as a possible route for its expansion effort. Alexander Gardner recorded this scene of the railroad survey party working in the boulder-strewn arroyo, with the Sandia foothills to the left and the north flank of the Manzanos to the right.

Although no railroad line was ever completed through Tijeras Canyon, its importance as a travel corridor has grown markedly over the years. A two-lane highway was completed in 1925, and twelve years later it was paved with asphalt when it became part of a realignment of the famed US Route 66. In 1950, the canyon's road was modernized to a four-lane divided highway, and two decades later I-40 was completed. With so many trees blocking the view today from Gardner's vantage point, I decided to make my photograph from a short distance up the steep arroyo slope. In this scene, high-speed traffic is streaming along I-40, which is paralleled by NM 333, today's designation for this stretch of old US 66.

Isleta Pueblo Church, 1867

Portions of the foundation and walls of the church at Isleta Pueblo have been dated to around 1613, supporting claims that it is the oldest church in New Mexico. A group of Isleta residents and the church's priest, believed to be the Reverend J. B. Brun, struck an intriguing pose in 1867 for this fine photograph by Alexander Gardner. Mud-plaster had been applied to about half of the church's front sometime not long before this picture was taken. The line indicating where the plastering job left off is apparent. The convento (priests' quarters), with its three arched entryways and roofed balcony, is attached to the church.

In the years between Gardner's and my photographs, the church at Isleta Pueblo underwent several major architectural transformations. By the late 1890s, the last vestiges of the old convento, a couple of the adobe arches, had melted back to the ground. The last major remodeling was done in 1960, when the church assumed its current look. It was refreshed with a bright white plastering sometime not long before I made my shot. During the 1960 renovation, the log coffin of a priest who had been buried beneath the dirt sanctuary floor in 1756 resurfaced, as it had about every generation since its burial. This time the remains were re-interred beneath a substantial concrete floor.

Rio Grande and Sandia Mountains, circa 1935

T. Harmon Parkhurst made this view of the Rio Grande and the distant Sandia Mountains from near the ruins of Kuaua Pueblo. Four centuries earlier, in 1540, Coronado and his fellow conquistadores arrived in this area at the outset of their quest for the fabled riches of Quivira and established a winter headquarters—either at Kuaua or at another nearby pueblo. The wooden bridge seen here provided the river crossing for the road connecting the Rio Grande valley with northwestern New Mexico.

When archaeologists excavated Kuaua Pueblo, at today's Coronado State Monument, they discovered and preserved one of the country's finest examples of prehistoric art —a kiva wall lined with layer upon layer of adobe plaster, many of the layers adorned with beautiful, multicolored murals. Parkhurst was somehow able to shoot from a slightly higher vantage point than I was. My photograph, however, benefits from the colorful cottonwoods that have grown up along the river over the last several decades. The highway bridge was moved south a short distance to its present location, and I was unable to find any sign of the old wooden structure.

Santa Fe–Albuquerque Highway, 1937

Photograph by Edward Weston

Edward Weston, one of the great modernists of American photography, captured this scene of two-lane US 66 between Santa Fe and Albuquerque during a 1937 visit to New Mexico. Earlier in the year, Weston had been the first photographer to be awarded a prestigious Guggenheim Foundation fellowship. He decided to use his two-thousand-dollar stipend for a year-long photographic trip through the West. Charis Wilson, who was soon to become his second wife, accompanied him on this trip and later wrote about this highway scene, "Most New Mexico roads look as though they had been laid out with a ruler and pencil in a New York office; with apparent disregard for topographical features, they persistently follow the course that was once considered to be the shortest distance between two points. . . . As we drove south to Albuquerque, Edward made a negative of one of these long straight ribbons of highway."

The hill from which Weston photographed was removed when four lanes of I-25 replaced the old two-lane highway. An equally notable change is San Felipe Pueblo's Casino Hollywood—part of the recent and pervasive Indian gaming phenomenon that is changing the roadside and cultural landscapes of Indian New Mexico. I had the good fortune of speaking directly with Charis Wilson about her description of Weston's scene, written more than sixty years ago. She recalled details of the place as if she had just driven the old highway. When New Mexico Magazine published Weston's image, she noted, "The editors showed their sense of delicacy by performing a Caesarean section on the print to remove the wrecked car in the foreground." She was pleased when I mentioned that the image would be reproduced here in its entirety.

Sandia Mountains from Albuquerque, 1917

U.S. Geological Survey (USGS) geologist N. H. Darton photographed this view of the Sandia Mountains from "Tijeras Road, about 10 miles east of Albuquerque," according to the photo caption in the USGS photo library. As far as the eye can see—from Darton's camera location all the way to the west face of the Sandias —the land was undeveloped in 1917. At that time Albuquerque had a population of less than fifteen thousand, and development had yet to reach much beyond the immediate valley of the Rio Grande.

With Darton's old photo in hand, I drove along I-40 and several Albuquerque streets trying to find the matching perspective of the mountains. This kind of shot is tough to replicate, with nothing in the foreground to help with alignment. I kept coming back to one area, near the interstate, which is now home to this city-owned skateboard park, and I decided to do my shot here. With my camera mounted on a twelve-foot-tall tripod, and the shot composed, I then waited for a good separation of action throughout the scene before making the exposure. I spent at least an hour watching these kids do their fantastic tricks on all sorts of wheeled devices—skateboards, bicycles, in-line skates, and scooters. Had I been able to shoot from a hundred feet higher, Albuquerque's urban development would have been seen spreading all the way to the mountains.

The mountains of northern New Mexico do not simply die away at their margins. To the west and northwest, especially, they shelve off into sheer-sided plateaus and ragged mesas scored by deep canyons. The tall pines and firs of the mountains also give way—first to the shrubby piñons and junipers that dot the higher plateaus, then to the sagebrush, grass, and greasewood of the vast, westward-reaching expanses of open country.

This huge northwestern part of New Mexico is a land of arid and semiarid plateaus extending into Arizona, Utah, and Colorado in long, sweeping vistas. Out along such highways as US 550 and I-40 (the successor of Route 66), numerous flat-topped mesas are always in view, and in the distance often a shadowed bulwark of cliffs is to be seen, or the stairstepping edges of giant plateaus. And over everything are vaulted skies that dazzle the land with light.

Closer at hand, the scale of things is often different. The land is intricately sculptured, most of it sandstone colored in shades of orange and red, as near Gallup, or in tans and tawny browns, as at Chaco Canyon and along the San Juan River. Clay badlands dominate the landscape in other places, all white, black, and purple, as at the Bisti/De-Na-Zin Wilderness. There are also monumental remains of volcanic activity, such as the lava flows of El Malpaís and the ancient cores of Mount Taylor and Ship Rock.

This area is New Mexico's portion of the Colorado Plateau, so named because all the land ultimately drains to the Colorado River. The waterways, however, are chiefly dry arroyos that may run a thunderstorm's torrent only on rare occasions. Notwithstanding the scarcity of precipitation, water is the operative agent here. Geologists knew early on that the mighty sculpturing of this land was the result of erosion, accomplished primarily by what little rain there is, assisted by frost and gravity—but hardly at all by wind, contrary to common belief. The weaker rocks and fractured rocks erode away most readily, though yet very slowly, leaving miles of free-standing cliffs and spires and slopes of tumbled, broken rock, together with occasional arches, windows, and pedestal rocks.

The more outstanding of these sculptured landmarks have always been irresistible, whether for prehistoric Indians, geologists, or photographers. Hence these pages include paired photos of Ship

NORTHWESTERN PLATEAU COUNTRY

Arch Rock, Arch Rock Canyon, 1907

Rock, the Navajo Church, El Morro, Pierced Rock, Venus Needle, the Gallup Hogback, and several other buttes and cliffs.

≈   ≈   ≈   ≈

The Colorado Plateau is the ancestral homeland of the Navajo Indians, and also of the Pueblo Indians, or Ancestral Puebloans, before they migrated over a period of centuries to the Rio Grande. Now only the Hopi pueblos of Arizona and three New Mexico pueblos —Zuni, Acoma, and Laguna—remain within the extent of the plateau. But there are countless ruins of old abandoned pueblos and occasional cliff dwellings, especially at Chaco Canyon.

It was the land, the Indians, and the prehistoric ruins that drew early photographers to the northwestern part of New Mexico. All three subjects were the interest, first, of the roving geological and geographical survey expeditions sent to the West by the federal government in the 1870s and 1880s. The personnel of each survey usually included just a single photographer, but the images made by these men were notable, for one reason because almost everything they pictured was being photographed for the first time.

The earliest of such men to work in New Mexico was Timothy H. O'Sullivan, the photographer for the Wheeler survey in 1873 and 1874. O'Sullivan spent a lot of time photographing in the pueblos north of Santa Fe and among the Hopis in Arizona. He is represented in our photos of northwestern New Mexico by a shot of Inscription Rock (see p. 84). O'Sullivan was always selective about camera angles and composition, wanting to maximize the drama of his scenes.

John K. Hillers (1843–1925) was also an experienced outdoor photographer. A veteran of Major John Wesley Powell's Grand Canyon explorations, Hillers had been photographing scenery and Indians for a decade at the time he toured parts of New Mexico in 1879 and 1880. He also photographed in New Mexico on later occasions, such as when he made the photos included here from atop the Gallup Hogback (see pp. 74 and 75).

And then there was the redoubtable William Henry Jackson (1843–1942). When he first came to New Mexico, Jackson was the photographer for the Hayden survey, making pictures mostly in Wyoming and Colorado. In 1877 Jackson photographed scenes in several New Mexico Indian pueblos, including Laguna and Acoma, and he also visited the great ruins of Chaco Canyon, which at the time had been seen by very few. Unfortunately, he experimented at the Chaco with a newly introduced dry-emulsion material that did not need to be developed immediately, and he was greatly disappointed to find later that all his exposures turned out blank. Hence, while photos of the Chaco ruin of Pueblo Bonito are included here (on pp. 70 and 72), they are photos made some twenty years after Jackson's visit, one by archaeologist George Pepper and one by journalist-photographer Charles F. Lummis.

Then, in 1879, the U.S. Geological Survey (USGS) was established to consolidate the several earlier surveys. Working for the USGS was another of Major Powell's associates, Captain Clarence E. Dutton (1841–1912), a geologist of unusual ability and eloquence. Most of the photographs attributed to him on these pages (see pp. 76, 78, 80, 85) show landforms and scenes of the Mount Taylor–Zuni Mountains area—products of Dutton's reconnaissance in 1884.

In another generation or two, the leadership of geologic studies in New Mexico was passed to such men as Nelson Horatio Darton (1865–1948). N. H. Darton was an especially productive scholar of things geologic. During a fifty-year career at USGS, his many explorations, reports, publications, and maps provided new, basic information about the geology and resources of New Mexico and of several other states. He also made his own photographs at least on occasion, as exemplified by his 1901 exposures in the Gallup area (see p. 73).

Four Corners Monument, 1925

In 1875, U.S. Deputy Surveyor Chandler Robbins surveyed the boundary between the New Mexico and Arizona Territories and left behind a survey monument marking the point common to the New Mexico, Arizona, Utah, and Colorado Territories. The stone-pile monument shown here was probably built in 1899, when government surveyors working in southeastern Utah found that Robbins' monument had been disturbed. Situated in remote and desolate country on a low rise near the San Juan River, the Four Corners Monument has been built and rebuilt several times over the years—but always in the same location.

In 1962, the Bureau of Land Management and the Bureau of Indian Affairs built a concrete pad around the Four Corners Monument and included, in its corresponding quadrant, each state's name in tile and official seal in bronze. By this time, the Four Corners spot had become a popular tourist attraction, offering visitors the unique opportunity to stand in four states at once. In 1992, representatives from all four states, the Navajo and Ute Mountain Ute Nations, and various government agencies, along with several hundred guests, including me, gathered to dedicate another new monument and its surrounding plaza, shown here. The man in this photograph is a European visitor having his four-state souvenir picture taken by a traveling companion.

Colorado–New Mexico Boundary, 1902

In 1868 Ehud N. Darling was contracted by the General Land Office to survey and mark with monuments the thirty-seventh parallel, thereby establishing on the ground the boundary between the Colorado and New Mexico Territories. Darling's survey traversed three hundred and thirty-one miles and crossed rugged mountainous terrain. Some thirty years later, an inspection of the boundary revealed that many of Darling's monuments had been destroyed. Colorado unilaterally decided to establish a new boundary, but the federal government stepped in and ordered a new survey, for which one Howard B. Carpenter was hired. In this 1902 photograph, Carpenter's crew is encamped north of Shiprock at an astronomical survey station with equipment for making celestial observations used in determining latitude and longitude.

Most of the New Mexico–Colorado boundary established by Carpenter's survey was north of the line that Darling had laid down. This meant that a generous slice of Colorado, including three towns and five post offices, would be transferred to New Mexico. Colorado, by then a state, protested, and after many years of uncertainty in the status of the boundary, the U.S. Supreme Court in 1925 decided in favor of Colorado. The boundary would revert back to Darling's 1868 line. The Court ordered that all of Carpenter's monuments, including the one shown in the 1902 photograph, be destroyed, and that a resurvey of Darling's line should be undertaken. The landscape here has changed very little, with the exception of the high-tension power lines traversing the scene.

Ship Rock, circa 1914

One of the most famous natural landmarks of the Four Corners area, Ship Rock rises eighteen hundred feet above the surrounding terrain. It was called the Needle by Captain J. F. McComb in 1860, but the name Ship Rock began appearing on topographical maps around 1870. The Navajos call it Rock with Wings (Tsé Bit' A'i), referring to the volcanic dikes that radiate out, winglike, from the main formation. Seen here with two Navajo men on horseback, Ship Rock is sacred to the Navajos, who have a number of myths and ceremonies associated with it.

The erosion and weathering of landforms such as Ship Rock are very slow-acting, and this scene appears to have changed little over the years. Ship Rock is the neck of an ancient volcano that last erupted around thirty million years ago. It was formed at least two thousand feet below the ground surface and was slowly revealed over the millennia as erosion stripped away the surrounding surface material. Local Navajos still sometimes ride horses in the area, although pickup trucks are the much-preferred mode of transportation throughout Navajo country today.

Farmington, circa 1880

Shot from a hill at the east end of town, looking down the broad valley of the San Juan River, this is Farmington's earliest known photograph, and it captures the small town in its infancy. Although stockmen had come for many years to this rich agricultural area near the confluence of the Animas, La Plata, and San Juan Rivers to buy produce and forage, Farmington was not formally established until 1879. According to notes on the back of this photograph, which I found in the Farmington Museum collection, the adobe building on the right served as the town's first schoolhouse and was also utilized by a local preacher named Griffin.

New Mexico is rich in many natural resources, including oil and natural gas. For the past several decades, the Farmington area's economy has been highly dependent on business related to the extraction of these resources from the nearby San Juan Basin. Having prospered in its role as the primary center of commerce servicing the vast Four Corners country, Farmington has come a long way in the hundred-and-twenty-year span represented by these photographs.

Aztec, circa 1910

When the time came to name their town, early residents of Aztec borrowed the name of the long-abandoned Ancestral Puebloan village located just across the Animas River. In 1890, Aztec was named the seat of San Juan County, which had been carved from Rio Arriba County a few years earlier. Farmers and ranchers came from miles around in the San Juan Basin to do business here, and businesses along Main Street prospered. Most of the buildings seen in this view were constructed between 1903 and the time the photograph was taken, a few years after the 1905 arrival of the railroad.

Aztec has the best-preserved downtown section of century-old buildings that I encountered during the course of this project. A couple of the buildings were lost to fire over the years, but most have survived. Aztec lists an impressive seventy-eight structures on the National Register of Historic Places. My parents, who are window-shopping at the second building from the left in this scene, and I marveled at some of the building details we could still identify from the old photograph. Although Aztec lost its railroad, it gained the important commerce that accompanied the discovery of oil and gas in the San Juan Basin.

Aztec Ruins, circa 1905

Aztec Ruins National Monument

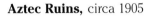

This pre-excavation view of the West Ruin portion of Aztec Ruins was shot by George Beam, who photographed for the Denver & Rio Grande Western Railroad in the early twentieth century. Aztec was built by Ancestral Puebloan people in the early 1100s—not by the Aztecs of Mexico, as was believed by early Anglo settlers who named the ruins. When the first recorded visitor, a geologist named Dr. John Newberry, viewed the ruins in 1859, he saw walls that stood twenty-five feet high in places and many undisturbed rooms. Sadly, vandals, pot hunters, and locals in search of free building materials caused considerable damage to the site during the half-century that followed.

Aztec Ruins came under the protection of the American Museum of Natural History in 1916, the same year that the young archaeologist Earl Morris began a multiyear project of excavating and stabilizing the West Ruin and nearby plaza. In 1923 Aztec Ruins became a national monument, and a few years later, Morris returned to Aztec and oversaw the reconstruction of the great kiva that he had previously excavated. One of the highlights for today's visitors to Aztec Ruins National Monument is to walk down into this amazing structure, the Southwest's only restored great kiva, to marvel at its engineering and ponder its significance. Close inspection of the walls reveals some of the same stone blocks in both views.

For a few years in the early 1900s, John and Louisa Wetherill ran a small trading post here on Alamo Wash, about fifteen miles north of Chaco Canyon, where John's brother, Richard, also ran a post. The trading post at Ojo Alamo was affiliated with the Hyde Exploring Expedition, a privately funded archaeological enterprise that sponsored much of the early discovery work in the Four Corners country. The Navajo residents of the badland country around Ojo Alamo would trade wool, mutton, and handmade blankets for staples such as flour, coffee, and sugar. The tents and buggy in this scene belong to a U.S. Geological Survey field party that was camped near the store.

*The large cottonwood tree still stands near the spring at Ojo Alamo, but the trading post is long gone. A makeshift corral fence—constructed of old bed springs, bald tires, and a hodgepodge of tree branches— now encompasses the spring and the site's namesake tree (*ojo alamo *is Spanish for "cottonwood spring"). Ojo Alamo is surrounded by the colorful badlands and sculpted rocks of today's Bisti/De-Na-Zin Wilderness. Dinosaurs lived in this area around seventy million years ago, and Alamosaurus was named for the spring, near which this fossil dinosaur was discovered. When I signed the trailhead register at the start of my exploratory hike to this site, I noticed that John Wetherill's great-grandson had ventured into the wilderness with a similar goal just days earlier.*

Pueblo Bonito at Chaco Canyon, circa 1898

George Pepper, a Harvard student, and Richard Wetherill, a rancher-turned-archaeologist, working under the auspices of the American Museum of Natural History and with the financial support of the Hyde Exploring Expedition, undertook the first major archaeological excavation at Chaco Canyon's Pueblo Bonito. Built over a three-hundred-year period ending in the early 1100s, Pueblo Bonito consisted of nearly seven hundred rooms and many kivas. For four field seasons, starting in 1896, Pepper, Wetherill, and a crew of Navajo laborers worked to remove accumulated dirt and debris from rooms and collected valuable artifacts, which at the end of the first season filled a railroad freight car. The single-room structure next to the wagon was the expedition office and Wetherill Trading Post, built onto Pueblo Bonito's imposing north wall. Pepper photographed this scene from atop the nearby mesa.

Chaco Culture National Historical Park

Pueblo Bonito is arguably the most impressive of all the Ancestral Puebloan structures that are known today. It is also enigmatic. Pueblo Bonito's population was just a fraction of its capacity. Most archaeologists now believe that Chaco Canyon was primarily a ceremonial center rather than a utilitarian residential complex. But much remains to be learned about the phenomenon of Chaco. Neil Judd conducted additional excavations at Pueblo Bonito in the 1920s and today's visitors to Chaco Culture National Historical Park can enjoy exploring the rooms and peering into kivas that were uncovered by the efforts of these archaeologists. Richard Wetherill's trading post is gone, and he is buried a short distance from this scene, having been shot and killed in Chaco in 1910.

Threatening Rock and Pueblo Bonito, 1901

When the Ancestral Puebloan residents of Chaco Canyon built Pueblo Bonito, they selected a site close to the base of the canyon's sheer northern cliffs. Over the years, erosion undercut a hundred-and-fifty-foot-long section of cliff above the east end of the pueblo. Sensing the threat this massive rock presented, the Chacoans attempted to stabilize it with a masonry buttress and support timbers. For added protection, apparently, they placed prayer sticks into the rock's crevices. During Richard Wetherill's time at Chaco, this rock was known as the Elephant. Local Navajos called Pueblo Bonito by a name that means "the house where the rocks are propped up."

On January 22, 1941, Threatening Rock—a name given by the National Park Service—came crashing down on Pueblo Bonito. The thirty-thousand-ton rock crushed a section of the pueblo's multistory north wall and heavily damaged or destroyed some sixty-five rooms. Massive pieces of Threatening Rock still lie in a jumbled pile, exactly the way they fell six decades ago. Today's visitors to Chaco can tour Pueblo Bonito by walking a trail that meanders through this rubble on its way through the complex. Whether the Chacoans' efforts at stabilizing Threatening Rock delayed its collapse will never be known. However, the rock stayed upright for nearly eight centuries after Pueblo Bonito was abandoned.

Gallup and the Hogback, 1901

When U.S. Geological Survey geologist N. H. Darton photographed the railroad tracks and Hogback on the east edge of Gallup, the tracks had been in place for twenty years. Prior to the railroad's arrival, however, Gallup was little more than the Blue Goose Saloon—a combination stage stop, saloon, and store. The town name came with the train—David Gallup was paymaster of the Atlantic and Pacific Railroad and rail workers would talk about "going to Gallup's" on payday. The same year that Darton shot this photograph, Gallup became the seat of newly formed McKinley County.

Gallup has grown considerably since its early days. From the original downtown area, businesses have spread both east and west along the route of old US 66, seen in this photo. Gallup is an important trade and tourism center for much of western New Mexico. People come from the world over to enjoy a taste of American Indian cultural traditions that are so much a part of the region. I scrambled up the side of the segment of the Hogback that is sandwiched between I-40 and the railroad tracks to match Darton's photograph. After composing my shot, I waited for a train to come along and captured, in a slow-shutter-speed blur, the locomotives of an eastbound freight.

Gallup Hogback Panoramic, 1881

John Hillers, photographing for the U.S. Geological Survey in 1881, climbed the Hogback east of Gallup and made this panoramic sequence of five images documenting a greater-than-180-degree view. The scene includes the Gallup area at about the time the railroad tracks were being laid: the cliffs of the Red Rock escarpment, prominent Pyramid Rock and Navajo Church, the gently rolling piñon and juniper country around Fort Wingate, the northern flank of the Zuni Mountains, and the Hogback itself—both north and south of Hillers' vantage point.

By studying the old photos and the area's topographic maps, I felt I had identified Hillers' vantage point for these views. I was pleased, therefore, when I scrambled to the top of the Hogback and was rewarded with the view I sought. This scene is considerably changed today. Gallup has become a fair-sized city, I-40 and the railroad now pass across the entire view, a refinery stands in front of Pyramid Rock, and munitions storage bunkers dot the Fort Wingate landscape. Details of the Hogback have changed little, if at all. The U.S. Geological Survey's annual report for 1884–1885 includes a fine fold-out panoramic drawing of this same view, likely the work of William Henry Holmes and most certainly based on Hillers' sequence of photographs.

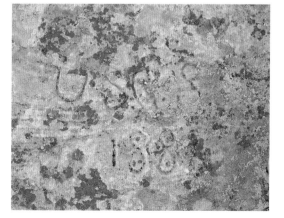

While setting up my camera to record the panoramic sequence, something at the very top of the Hogback, perhaps a hundred feet away, caught my eye. I walked closer and saw, cut into the top face of a sloping sandstone slab, a lichen-encrusted inscription, "USGS 1881." I wondered whether John Hillers himself had registered his agency's visit to the top of the Hogback.

Todilto Park and Venus Needle, 1884

The famous western geologist Captain Clarence E. Dutton recorded this view of the sheer sandstone cliffs surrounding the open grasslands of Todilto Park on the Navajo Indian Reservation. Isolated Venus Needle, seen at the far right, rises two hundred feet above the surrounding terrain. Tohdildonih Wash meanders across the middle ground of this scene, draining the western slope of the Chuska Mountains, just out of view to the right. The Navajo name todilto *means "breaking out of the waters" and refers to a legendary lake that once occupied the area and was dramatically drained in a day—a real-world scenario that is partially corroborated by the area's geological record.*

Tohdildonih Wash has downcut dramatically into Todilto Park during the hundred and twenty years spanned by these two photographs. Dutton's vantage point has been eroded away, so I made my photograph from atop a steep, fifty-foot cutbank along the south side of the wash, as much as a hundred feet from where Dutton stood in 1880. The change in vegetation that has occurred over the years is striking—cottonwoods and invasive Russian olive now abound. A local Navajo man told me that his grandparents used to reminisce about the western movies that were filmed here—replete with Hollywood cowboys and wagon trains passing through this very scene.

Hogback at Nutria, 1884

U.S. Geological Survey topographic parties mapping northwestern New Mexico in the early 1880s reported back to Washington, D.C., that they had encountered a number of striking landforms and interesting geologic situations. John Wesley Powell, the agency's director, asked Captain Clarence E. Dutton to spend a field season studying the area, with a particular focus on Mount Taylor and its environs. During his travels, Dutton photographed this view of the upturned strata of Dakota sandstone along the Rio Nutria, a few miles west of the Continental Divide. In his 1885 report, Mount Taylor and the Zuni Plateau, *Dutton describes this scene with the words: "The great flexure seems to roll up out of the earth with its beds standing nearly vertically and with the broken edges of the horizontal strata walling against them."*

In the eighteenth and nineteenth centuries, many Zuni Pueblo residents established small, seasonally occupied satellite settlements in outlying areas around the main village. Upper Nutria, located near this scene, was one. These sites helped the Zunis to utilize some of the more productive land for grazing livestock and growing crops. In the 1930s, several Zuni springs, including the one near Upper Nutria, were developed, and reservoirs were constructed to provide the farmers with more reliable water sources. I photographed drought-depleted Nutria Diversion Reservoir, complete with a sky similar to Dutton's, during the dry summer of 2002. On the far shore a vehicle tows a water tank, which a local sheepherder is filling from the reservoir to water his flock.

Feather Rock and Pierced Rock, 1884

Captain Clarence E. Dutton photographed this scene immediately downstream from the confluence of the Rio Pescado and Rio Nutria, where these two tributaries join to form the Zuni River. Here, the Zuni sandstone has been eroded, revealing a striated cliff with a natural arch piercing a rock fin, and an isolated outlying spire. I found several late-nineteenth-century photographs of this spire, variously labeled as the Sentinel Lion, Devil's Thumb, and Needle Rock. The subject's location was often identified as Zuni Pass. That none of these place names is in use today complicated my efforts in finding this location.

A Zuni legend about the Zuni Salt Lake says, in part, that when the Salt Mother became dismayed with abuse of the salt resource she was providing, she departed her Zuni sacred spring home and moved south, to the lake. She wanted to show the people where she had gone so she left visible markers along the way. Passing through the edge of the mesa seen here, the Salt Mother created the opening in the rock fin. She also took an eagle feather from her headdress, which turned to stone when she planted it in the ground. These two features are now known as Pierced Rock, high up on the cliff, and Feather Rock. The environmental health and cultural integrity of the Zuni Salt Lake area is greatly threatened today by plans to develop a coal mine nearby.

Navajo Church, 1901

Standing above the surrounding terrain, Navajo Church has long been a prominent landmark for travelers passing through western New Mexico. It has also been a popular photography subject through the years. I found many fine old views of this sandstone formation as I searched through collections of historical photographs. Many of these pictures included the unusual mushroom rock in the foreground—a wonderful geologic oddity that caught my eye as it did the eyes of several photographers more than a hundred years ago.

Today, Navajo Church, which is also known as Church Rock, can be reached by a hiking trail in Red Rock Park. A few Navajo homesites are scattered about on the north side of the formation. Nearby, my father and I found a large concrete water-well pad that impressed us with the effort its construction in such a remote place must have entailed. The area still has a faraway and timeless feel, much as I imagine it had for the early photographers and visitors who ventured here.

Cubero, circa 1885

The village of Cubero, located a few miles west of Laguna Pueblo, has its roots in the early Spanish days of the area. It was probably named for Pedro Rodríguez Cubero, who served as governor of New Mexico following Diego de Vargas. When Mexico claimed the region in 1821, the village prospered from the opening of trade routes. During its territorial days, Cubero was a temporary home to U.S. soldiers who were involved in the campaign to contain the Navajo Indians, whose name for Cubero means "water in the crevice." The side of the village's Catholic church appears at the very right edge of Ben Wittick's photograph. Notice the clothes drying on the line at the left.

Twenty-first-century Cubero is a rather quiet place. The church is still in the same location, but cottonwood trees as well as piñon and juniper have taken hold during the past hundred-plus years. These photographs, which include a fine view of Mount Taylor in the distance, were made from near the top of a hill on the village's south edge. The hill is strewn with dark volcanic boulders of various shapes and sizes. Several of the boulders, particularly in the right foreground, can be matched from one photo to the other. Perhaps the man in Wittick's photograph leaned against his prop a bit too hard—that same boulder now lies on its side.

Inscription Rock, 1873

Timothy H. O'Sullivan was the expedition photographer for one of the great geographical surveys of the West when he photographed this natural and cultural landmark in northwestern New Mexico. Visitors had inscribed the base of this sandstone prominence, also called El Morro ("headland"), with names and figures for nearly a thousand years: Ancestral Puebloans, Spanish colonizers, nineteenth-century explorers, military personnel, and emigrants on their way west.

El Morro National Monument

El Morro National Monument was designated in 1906 to protect the stone carvings of Inscription Rock. Today's visitors can walk a paved trail to see the cliff-side entries and reach the top of the monolith, where they can view the ruins of Atsina Pueblo, built around 1275. When I set out to replicate O'Sullivan's image, I was surprised to find that he had used a very wide-angle lens. His up-close and upward-looking composition imparts a powerful dynamic to the scene.

Spanish Inscription at Inscription Rock, 1873

New Mexico's governor from 1618 to 1625, Don Juan de Eulate, visited this natural stop on the Zuni-Acoma Trail in the same year as the Pilgrims' arrival at Plymouth and left this rather self-serving Spanish inscription, which translates: "I am the captain General of the Provinces of New Mexico for the King our Lord, passed by here on the return from the pueblos of Zuni on the twenty-ninth of July the year 1620, and put them at peace at their humble petition, they asking favor as vassals of his Majesty and promising anew their obedience, all of which he did, with clemency, zeal, and prudence, as a most Christian-like gentleman extraordinary and gallant soldier of enduring and praised memory." The Spanish word for "gentleman" was gouged out—perhaps by someone who took exception to this characterization of Eulate—sometime before 1849, when R. H. Kern made a detailed drawing of the inscription.

Eulate's inscription is now a fenced-in stop on the interpretive trail that leads visitors past the rock carvings. As I left the stop and hurried along to photograph another inscription before the low winter sun disappeared behind Inscription Rock, something on the cliff face caught my eye. I stopped dead in my tracks. There, framed by the tangled branches of an old juniper tree and side-lit by the bright sun, was this carving (at right), left by photographer Timothy H. O'Sullivan as a record of his 1873 visit.

Mesa Chivato View, 1884

The U.S. Geological Survey's annual report for 1884–1885 includes a rendering of this photograph as one of its plates. In the report's text, Captain Clarence E. Dutton describes this easterly view from the edge of Mesa Chivato as " …a fine one and in some respects extraordinary. The edge of the mesa suddenly descends by a succession of ledges and slopes nearly 2,000 feet into the rugged and highly diversified valley-plain below." The prominent, dark-colored formations seen in the distance are volcanic necks located in the Rio Puerco Valley, which boasts the greatest concentration and best examples of such formations in the world.

To reach this vantage point, I climbed more than a thousand vertical feet up the side of Mesa Chivato. My ascent involved hiking on a long-abandoned and arroyo-rough prospector's jeep trail, as well as some cross-country scrambling. The view that awaited me was sublime and timeless, a scene changed very little in nearly a hundred and twenty years—except for today's high-tension power lines. My emotions that day were heavily burdened by the morning's news of the tragic loss of the space shuttle Columbia. And, immediately prior to taking this picture, I said a prayer for the seven courageous astronauts and their families. It dawned on me later that less than five hours before I photographed this scene, Columbia had flown nearly directly over this place, as its disaster was unfolding on approach to Cape Canaveral. I also learned that the muffled boom heard by my wife, Carolyn, and me while sipping coffee just before I left the house was indeed caused by Columbia.

NORTHEASTERN MOUNTAINS AND PLAINS

Fourth of July Celebration, Clayton, 1909

Northeastern New Mexico has been a gateway to the territory and state since the days of the Santa Fe Trail. Over the trail, entering New Mexico near its northeastern corner, came not only goods such as fabrics, glassware, and tools, but new people, new ideas, new institutions, and new technologies. Among the ideas and institutions were Anglo-American concepts of personal liberty and democratic government, arriving over the trail with General Stephen Watts Kearny's army in 1846. And one of the technologies was the railroad that eventually put the trail out of business.

Such things arrived via the trail's relatively level passage across the Great Plains of Kansas and eastern Colorado. But when trail drivers reached New Mexico, they came upon a more rough and varied land, one of pine-clad mountains and rocky mesas. Grassy expanses were broken by escarpments, and abrupt canyons incised every horizon.

This was not an easy land, not only because of rough terrain but because the climate and the mountains didn't provide enough water. The largest river, the Pecos, had only a modest flow, as likewise did the Canadian River. The Cimarron River, alongside the Cutoff branch of the Santa Fe Trail, sometimes had water, but it was not without reason that in New Mexico the stream was called the Dry Cimarron.

This meant that agriculture and livestock raising in New Mexico would have limitations, as they already did for the Hispanic people. New Mexico was too dry, some said. Naught but a desert, others said—a place unfit for habitation, where nothing would ever be achieved or accomplished.

Nevertheless, the imported people, ideas, and ideals found footholds in northeastern New Mexico and spread from there to the rest of the territory. The historical photographs on the following pages offer a sampling of what transpired and shortly came to be. Fort Union was established to guard the trail from Utes and Apaches, and, as it turned out, Confederates during the Civil War. The town of Raton grew around the spot chosen as a railroad division point. Las Vegas was a Hispanic village that in a few years was transformed into a good-sized town by the coming of the railroad. The coal mines at Dawson became perhaps New Mexico's first industrial enterprise of note, serving several railroads. Clayton became an Anglo-American center of ranching and farming, a typical example of communities that sprouted in all the Plains states and territories in the 1880s.

In addition, the photographs showing Montezuma Castle are reminders of an early time in the railroad history of the Southwest. The "castle" was built, was burned twice, and was rebuilt each time by the Santa Fe Railway as a sumptuous destination resort, located in a mountain canyon near the town of Las Vegas. The hotel would now appear to have been an early trial run for affluent tourism in the West—ultimately unsuccessful here—coming well before the same railroad built its famous hotels at the Grand Canyon, before Southern California became a tourist mecca, and of course long before Nevada's own city of Las Vegas was even a dot on a map.

ᐯ   ᐯ   ᐯ   ᐯ

The years following the Civil War brought enormous changes to New Mexico, and the single most important factor in all of the changes was the coming of the railroads. No other development or technology compared with the railroads in opening up the territory. The railroads transformed transportation, transformed the economy of the territory, and in the process transformed people's outlooks and aspirations.

Because of the railroads, natural resources that had been only latent became resources in fact—coal deposits, timberlands, farming and grazing lands, and ores of copper, silver, and gold. All such things had new values when they could be transported and linked to markets. Similarly, new goods of every sort could be brought to consumers. Thus the railroads brought new opportunities into being.

The first railroad to enter New Mexico arrived in 1878, when the tracks of the Atchison, Topeka & Santa Fe Railway were constructed across Raton Pass. Within the next thirty months, a thousand miles of track were built in the territory, and in subsequent years another two thousand miles were built. The Santa Fe's tracks were extended the length of New Mexico to connect with a Southern Pacific track, thus completing the second transcontinental route. Eventually the Santa Fe's main line reached westward from Albuquerque, creating another route across the continent, from Chicago to Los Angeles.

ᐯ   ᐯ   ᐯ   ᐯ

Railroad building also brought to the territory Alexander Gardner, who may have been the first truly professional photographer to visit New Mexico. Gardner (1821–1882) was a Scot who had immigrated to the United States and had gained experience taking battlefield pictures for Matthew Brady, the well-known photographer of the Civil War.

Before the end of the war, however, Gardner opened his own studio in Washington, D.C. There, in April 1865, he made what proved to be the final photograph of Abraham Lincoln. As it happened, President Lincoln walked over to Gardner's studio from the White House, a few days following the war's end, to have his portrait made. Within another few days he was assassinated.

Some time later, Gardner gave up his studio and signed on as the photographer of an exploring party to determine a route for a railroad that was to extend from Kansas to California. The party traveled through New Mexico in 1867, more or less following the Santa Fe Trail, establishing the feasibility of a route that thirteen years later was indeed used by the Santa Fe Railway.

Gardner made photos all along and near the route, including numerous pictures of New Mexico scenes. Sometimes he included a horseman or a wagon to lend scale and visual interest, or to serve as a counterpoint to the vastness of the scene. Such inclusions, it has been suggested, may have expressed Gardner's own feeling of being engulfed by the empty land.

Galisteo, 1882

Ancestral Puebloan Indians inhabited the Galisteo Basin for centuries, and the petroglyphs they carved into the dark volcanic rocks are among the finest in the Southwest. One of their pueblos, known in Spanish Colonial times as Galisteo, was not far from where J. R. Riddle shot this photograph. By 1800, however, all of the area's pueblos had been abandoned. And in the mid-nineteenth century, Hispanic settlers moved into the area, established the village of Galisteo (seen here with its recently built church), and pastured herds of sheep among the deserted walls of the old pueblos.

Galisteo retains some of the feel of its early days, and the church still anchors the town center. However, the area has also become home to art galleries and luxury spas, while high-end homes dot the landscape around town. I made my photograph as the dark clouds of a fall thunderstorm skirted the town. J. R. Riddle must have shot his photograph from a rooftop, as was often done in the early days. I was unable to get as high a vantage point as he used, but I managed to get a similarly composed view.

Madrid, circa 1935

Madrid was founded in the late 1860s; by the late 1880s, the area's coal was being mined on a large scale. The Santa Fe Railway brought in a spur line to transport coal directly from the breaker shown at right. Then, for some thirty-five years beginning in 1919, Madrid was a company town: The Albuquerque and Cerrillos Coal Company ran the place, including nearly all the town's businesses and support infrastructure. Around the time that T. Harmon Parkhurst photographed this scene, Madrid was renowned for its elaborate display of electric Christmas lights that attracted thousands of viewers—even those aboard commercial airlines, whose pilots would sometimes alter course to allow passengers to observe the festive scene from above.

As natural gas and diesel fuel displaced coal for many of the country's energy needs, Madrid's coal mining activity declined. Finally, in 1954, the mines were closed and the town was put up for sale—as a package offering. No buyers came forward, though, and in 1975 the remaining houses were sold off to individuals. The coal breaker and power plant structures, prominent in the old view, are gone now, but many of the company houses still stand and have become residences or art galleries. I shot my photograph on the Fourth of July, a holiday that had been celebrated in extraordinary style during the town's glory days.

Madrid Baseball Park, circa 1927

Over the years, the Madrid Miners baseball team won many Minor League pennants. Miners and semi-professional athletes played together on the team, which practiced and played to enthusiastic home-field crowds. Richard Melzer, in Madrid Revisited: Life and Labor in a New Mexico Mining Camp in the Years of the Great Depression, *recounts that eager fans would park their cars along the foul lines as early as 7 a.m. on game days to reserve good viewing for the afternoon's play. The Miners' home ballpark boasted New Mexico's first grandstand and electric night lights and scoreboard—powered by the nearby coal-mine generators.*

Activity at Madrid's ballpark today is a far cry from what it was three-quarters of a century ago. It's now more likely to be the venue for a music concert or special community event than for a hard-played ball game. There was not a soul around the early summer evening that I recorded my "now" rendition of this scene.

Pecos Pueblo and Church, 1880

The first church at Pecos Pueblo was completed in 1625. During the 1680 Pueblo Revolt, the Indians of Pecos burned the massive structure, but it was rebuilt in the eighteenth century and served the Catholic missionary effort in the area for many years. By 1800, however, the residents of Pecos Pueblo had been so beaten down by Comanche raids, disease, and the missionaries' demands that the people could no longer sustain themselves. A handful of survivors eventually left Pecos and moved to Jemez Pueblo, with whose people they shared a common language. This photograph of the ruined church and convento *(priests' quarters) documents an 1880 visit by the archaeologist Adolph Bandelier.*

Thirty-five years passed after Bandelier's visit to Pecos before Alfred Kidder would begin the laborious process of excavating and stabilizing the ruined pueblo and church. Kidder spent a dozen field seasons at Pecos, and his work profoundly influenced American archaeological practices. Among the finds was an underground ceremonial chamber, or kiva, seen here, with the ladder. Pecos residents had built this kiva amid the ruins of the church complex in an attempt to return to their own religion and to display their scorn for the missionaries. Even today, Pecos Pueblo, now a national historical park, has a wonderfully remote, ancient feeling.

Tecolote Creek, 1867

Alexander Gardner photographed this view of Tecolote Creek, south of Las Vegas, during a fifteen-month exploratory expedition for the Kansas-Pacific Railroad Company. The company had hired and outfitted a party of surveyors, engineers, topographers, support personnel, and a photographer to determine and document the best route to extend their tracks from western Kansas through New Mexico and on to California. A troop of thirty cavalrymen accompanied the party, primarily for protection against Apaches. Gardner's inclusion of the wagon, probably containing his portable darkroom, adds a pleasing manmade element to an otherwise natural landscape photograph.

Alexander Gardner's historical photograph intrigued me, so I decided to take on the challenge of finding this site. It took me a few trips to figure this scene out and, once I gained permission to go onto private ranchland—a process that involved an exciting encounter with a shotgun—I was able to walk right to the vantage point. Unfortunately, the exact view today is mostly blocked by piñon and juniper trees, so I had to shift several feet to the side from the rock outcrop where Gardner had obviously stood. As indicated by the creek-spanning bridge, a railroad did indeed run tracks across Tecolote Creek, but not until thirteen years after Gardner had made his photograph.

Las Vegas, 1867

Alexander Gardner recorded this view of Las Vegas just twenty-one years after Brigadier General Stephen Watts Kearny, at the advent of the Mexican War, arrived in town and claimed the entire region for the United States. Reportedly the oldest known photograph of Las Vegas, this scene includes the plaza area of West Las Vegas, with the Gallinas River channel meandering through the middle ground.

When I first scouted this scene, I decided that Gardner must have made his photograph from the rise where New Mexico Highlands University is located today—but trees and buildings completely blocked the way. During a subsequent visit, I was astounded to find that a campus construction project had opened up the view I needed. The hill from which both Gardner and I shot our pictures, a hundred and thirty years apart, was being cut back by construction equipment while I watched. The pile of excavated shale in my photograph mirrors the eroded debris mound in Gardner's scene. The Plaza Hotel, built in 1882, can be glimpsed through the trees near the center.

Montezuma Castle, circa 1900

A formally attired group posed in front of the hotel fountain, circa 1884.

The elaborate Montezuma Hotel was built in 1882 by the Atchison, Topeka & Santa Fe Railway as a getaway resort for wealthy patrons, who came via train on a short spur off the main line at Las Vegas. The structure burned to the ground less than two years later. Undaunted, Santa Fe management immediately began planning an even grander replacement, which opened just over a year later, in April 1885. But fire again gutted the Montezuma that summer. In the following year, the third and final rendition of the Montezuma Hotel—officially and appropriately named the Phoenix Hotel—arose from the ashes, as seen here in William Henry Jackson's photograph.

The third and final Montezuma Hotel building had a rather short-lived existence as a lodging establishment and closed its doors in the early 1900s. Since that time, the building has seen such divergent uses as a seminary and a movie set. For two decades now, the Montezuma Castle, as the structure has been known for many years, has served as the architectural heart of the Armand Hammer United World College of the American West. Students from around the world now reside, dine, and study here. The Castle recently underwent a major structural and cosmetic restoration project that returned the old building to its former status as a beautiful and functional showpiece. The increase in tree cover seen here is rather astounding; I was lucky to find a break in the trees to get my shot.

Gallinas Canyon and Montezuma, 1904

Over the centuries, the hot springs of Montezuma in Gallinas Canyon have attracted Indians, Hispanic settlers, travelers on the Santa Fe Trail, and tourists. Just up-canyon from the springs, early residents built dams to impound Gallinas Creek and create winter ice ponds. After being cut into blocks, the ice was stored in the icehouse that appears near the center of this photograph. Some of the ice was used at the Montezuma Hotel, the large structure at left-center, and the remainder was transported on a spur line of the Santa Fe Railway to Las Vegas and occasionally beyond.

Today, the icehouse is gone and the Montezuma Hotel has become the focal point of the United World College. The density of the coniferous forest on the canyon slopes has increased considerably during the century that has passed between these images. The suppression of forest fires and the curtailment of timber harvesting have resulted in a similar, usually unhealthy, forest densification in many of New Mexico's timbered areas.

Fort Union, 1866

Fort Union was established in 1851 to protect travelers and goods on the nearby Santa Fe Trail. The fort occupied two other sites before construction was begun in 1863 on the final and largest complex, which comprised three distinct facilities—the post, the quartermaster's depot, and the arsenal. The Fort Union Quartermaster's Depot was the distribution point for most military supplies in the Southwest. A sizable force of wagons, teamsters, and wagonmasters was required to transport these goods throughout the region. The wagons were maintained here in the mechanic's corral. Note the firefighting equipment near the center of the scene, just left of the well house.

Fort Union National Monument

Fort Union's utility was greatly diminished with the 1879 arrival of the railroad in New Mexico and the eventual abandonment of the Santa Fe Trail. The complex was finally ordered closed in 1891. Preservation efforts were begun some fifty years later, and the National Park Service took over ownership and management in the 1950s. The ruins have been stabilized, and efforts continue to be made to mitigate the effects of the elements. I made my photograph from as high as I could get on a very tall tripod. The rooftop from which the 1866 image was shot is now long gone.

Raton, circa 1884

Before the 1879 arrival of the Santa Fe Railway, Raton (then called Willow Springs) was a quiet forage station and watering place on the Santa Fe Trail's Mountain Branch. The railroad located a major repair facility here, and a demand for rail workers grew. Coal was discovered nearby and exploited, and ranching activities expanded throughout the region. Raton soon boasted a population of several thousand residents, and the downtown area grew quickly. J. R. Riddle's photograph, shot from Goat Hill, shows the prosperous downtown area, including the prominent railroad roundhouse and a broad view of the mesas to the east.

My search for Riddle's exact camera location was a challenge. I eventually determined that sometime in the past hundred-and-some years, a rockfall had toppled several of the rock ledges seen near the man in Riddle's photograph. Perhaps this happened during the construction of a hilltop parking area and lighted sign, which now broadcasts the town's name for miles around. The roundhouse is gone today, but many trains still pass through Raton, including the Amtrak passenger train seen here. Note how many more trees there are today than in Raton's early days.

Dawson, circa 1910

The coal-mining town of Dawson came into existence at the start of the twentieth century and lasted fifty years. Throughout its history, all residents of the community lived in company housing and were served by company stores.

Eventually the market for Dawson's coal dwindled, leading the last owners of the property to close the mines and completely raze the town. Today, the town cemetery is almost the only reminder of the once-busy community.

Dawson Coke Ovens, 1920

Charles Eddy, known for his land and railroad development efforts in many parts of New Mexico, built a hundred-and-thirty-two-mile rail line from Tucumcari to Dawson, and in 1901 bought the Dawson coal fields from rancher J. B. Dawson. Just four years later, Eddy turned a tidy profit by selling out to the long-established Phelps Dodge Corporation. The company town of Dawson grew in concert with the expansion of the mines, and by 1917 the population had grown to nearly six thousand. Dawson's coal was especially well-suited for coking, a process that was done in these coke ovens, numbering almost six hundred.

Dawson was the site of two tragic mining accidents, in 1913 and 1923, which together claimed the lives of three hundred and eighty-five miners. Visitors can walk through Dawson's cemetery today and see row upon row of crosses memorializing the victims. The Dawson mines were shut down in 1950, and the company town was closed. Residents left town with whatever they could salvage from the old buildings, and the last of the impressive coke ovens was demolished just recently. Dawsonites gather every two years at a reunion on the old townsite to reminisce about Dawson's glory days. I was warmly welcomed into the 2002 gathering by members of the visiting Martinez clan, a family of twelve siblings who were all born in Dawson and all delivered by the same company doctor.

Capulin Mountain, circa 1909

Capulin Volcano National Monument

Northeastern New Mexico's Capulin Mountain is a textbook example of a volcanic cinder cone. The eruption that created the cone occurred about fifty thousand years ago, making it one of the more recent in a series of volcanic events in this region that began perhaps ten million years ago. The smaller formation, seen here with the man on top, is called a "squeeze-up," formed when the top surface of a lava flow hardens and cracks, allowing pasty lava to squeeze through like toothpaste. The tall stone cairn was probably a marker used for surveying and mapping. W.T. Lee, a noted geologist with the U.S. Geological Survey and an early-day advocate of the use of aerial photography, made this photograph.

Capulin Mountain National Monument (in 1987, the name changed to Capulin Volcano National Monument) was created in 1916. A two-mile summit road—the slash seen here running across the mountain—was built in the 1920s. Visitors who drive to the top of the cone are treated to a fine view, reportedly encompassing five states on a clear day. They can also take a trail down into the crater or completely around the rim. The cone's slopes have experienced a substantial increase in tree cover over the years, and some of the squeeze-up's outer layers of lava have sloughed off since the historical photograph was taken.

Most people who live in arid lands are grouped along rivers and streams, or wherever nature or man has concentrated a water supply. This is the case in southeastern New Mexico, which is a huge, water-deficient area mostly at the southern margin of the Great Plains. Here the grasslands of the Plains give way to the deserts of West Texas and northern Mexico. Ecologists and biologists consider southeastern New Mexico part of the Chihuahuan Desert, with much of it drought-tolerant grassland but some of it clearly dominated by creosote bush, mesquite, and other xerophytic plants.

As it happens, the Pecos River threads its way right down the middle of the southeastern plains, and along the river lie the larger towns and small cities of the region: Roswell, Artesia, and Carlsbad. Irrigation agriculture and livestock raising are important here; major products include cattle, cotton, and chili.

Closer to New Mexico's boundary with Texas is another scatter of cities and towns: Clovis, Portales, Lovington, and Hobbs. Near Clovis, the farmlands are irrigated from wells, and specialty crops such as peanuts and pecans are possible. Dairies and feedlots also share the rural scene here, while near Hobbs the oil and gas wells of the Permian Basin are prominent in the landscape.

The land between the two populated areas is called the Llano Estacado, or Staked Plains, an almost flat, featureless expanse. Legend has it that early-day wayfarers in these parts had to pound stakes into the ground to keep themselves from becoming lost. Perhaps this was not only legend but truth, although another explanation for the name has to do with the exposed rock edges of the Llano, which in places look like palisades of gigantic stakes holding the plain above the surrounding land.

Southeastern New Mexico was far from the Rio Grande and largely beyond the reach of early Hispanic settlement. Most of the area was settled, instead, by people moving westward from Texas in the late 1800s and the first decades of the 1900s. Many were the families that came across the state line in open wagons, some of them trailing strings of horses or herds of cattle.

Some of these immigrants were entrepreneurs—Charles B. Eddy, J. J. Hagerman, Joseph C. Lea—whose surnames became those of towns and counties. Other settlers became figures of folklore:

SOUTHEASTERN MOUNTAINS AND DESERTS

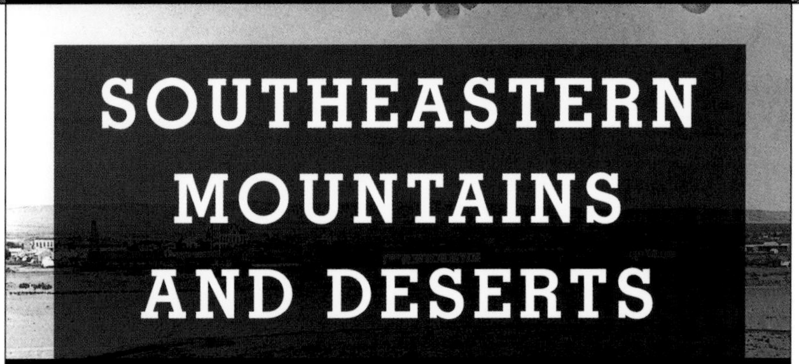

The Fledgling Town of Eddy, 1893

Pat Garrett, the sheriff of Lincoln County who killed Billy the Kid; John Chisum, a celebrated cattle king; Charles Goodnight and Oliver Loving, cattlemen known for trail-driving livestock to reach the railroads and help feed defeated Indian tribes.

Some of these men were also builders of irrigation works and railroads. One of the historical photographs remade by Bill Stone, for example, shows a major irrigation flume that was promoted by Eddy and Garrett (see p. 121).

≈ ≈ ≈ ≈

Southeastern New Mexico also has a long, irregular spine of mountains. Rising west of the Pecos Valley and draining to it, this spine consists of the Sacramento, Capitan, and Guadalupe Ranges, plus the gold-scattered Jicarilla Mountains on the north end. Together these ranges mark the eastward margins of what geologists know as the Basin and Range physiographic province, an enormous area of echeloned mountain ranges and arid basins that extends from southeastern New Mexico into California, Nevada, and Oregon.

The Sacramento Mountains are a remarkable assemblage of peaks, canyons, and forests. The mountains rise abruptly from the arid Tularosa Basin, then slope off for mile after mile eastward. The often-snowcapped Sierra Blanca Peak, the highest summit at 12,003 feet, is the southernmost glaciated mountain in the United States. It gives rise to the Rio Bonito (Pretty River) and the Rio Ruidoso (Noisy River), both of which are vital to towns and recreation areas on the eastern slopes.

Several historical photographs were made in the Sacramentos. Cloudcroft has long been a resort area (see p. 117). So has Ruidoso, shown here in photos of its birthplace at Dowlin's Mill (pp. 112, 113).

Lincoln is a historic village, focus of the bloody Lincoln County War of 1878–1881, but now a gentle place to visit (see p. 105). The photos of Fresnal Canyon (pp. 118, 119) provide glimpses of the steep road by which the mountains are ascended.

And because these mountains were the homeland of the Mescalero Apaches, in 1855 the U.S. Army began construction of Fort Stanton in an attempt to "control" the Indians and encourage non-Indian settlement. The fort was in a particularly favorable location, in a valley below the highest mountains, with plentiful pasture for cavalry horses and plentiful water from the Rio Bonito. Today the Mescalero Apaches still inhabit these mountains.

Off to the southeast of the Sacramentos is another part of the mountain spine, the Guadalupe Mountains. A quintessential desert range, barely softened by forest, the Guadalupes are all limestone strata that stand in bold relief. The strata are etched and riddled with caves, and deep within a lower ridge lie the Carlsbad Caverns, one of the world's great underground wonders.

≈ ≈ ≈ ≈

At 5:30 on the morning of July 16, 1945, the nuclear age was born—in New Mexico, in blinding light and searing heat. At that time and on that date, the first atomic bomb was test-exploded in the Jornada del Muerto at Trinity Site. Within a month the second and third bombs were delivered over the Japanese cities of Hiroshima and Nagasaki, bringing to an end the most terrible war in history.

At Trinity Site, the steel tower that held the bomb a hundred feet in the air was vaporized in an instant. But as the "then" and "now" photos show (pp. 106 and 107), the desert mountains beyond the site continue as lonely and mysterious as ever. Today at Trinity Site—and at Los Alamos, where the bomb was developed—one cannot help but think of contrasts and comparisons. In these same deserts and mountains, hardy Spanish explorers trudged in the 1540s. At Santa Fe, the Spaniards even established an outpost of medieval society. Yet here and now, these deserts and mountains are the sites of some of the world's most advanced and awesome scientific experiments, the vanguard explorations of modern times and of the future.

What are we to make of that?

Abó Canyon Railroad Bridge, 1905

Abó Pass, between the Manzano and Los Pinos Mountains, has long been an important travel corridor. The Ancestral Puebloan people, who painted and etched figures on nearby rock faces, crossed the pass on their way between the Rio Grande Valley and the salt lakes near Estancia. Centuries later, Santa Fe Railway surveyors determined that Abó Pass was the most practical route for linking the Rio Grande corridor with the main rail lines to the east. Seven arroyo-spanning bridges carry the tracks through Abó Canyon, as it drops from the pass down to the eastern flank of the Rio Grande. This photograph records the 1905 construction of the westernmost of these bridges.

Abó Canyon attracts railroad aficionados with the chance to watch long trains crossing scenic bridges in a beautiful desert canyon setting. I saw no fewer than a half-dozen trains in the two hours I spent when I first scouted this scene. Unfortunately, photography conditions that day were unfavorable. When I returned to make this photograph, not a train was to be seen—not until I had packed up my camera gear and started hiking back to my vehicle. At least I made it back on the road before the storm hit.

Lincoln, circa 1886

Settled in 1849 by Hispanic villagers from the Manzano Mountains area, Lincoln is best known for its center-stage role in the violent Lincoln County War. Peppered with political corruption, this conflict was a struggle between local business alliances for dominance in the region's ranching, banking, and retail endeavors. Billy the Kid was involved in the war, and later, in 1881, he was returned to Lincoln to await execution following his conviction for the murder of Sheriff William Brady. However, he managed to escape from the county courthouse (the large building in the center of this J. R. Riddle photograph) by killing two deputies.

A large number of Lincoln's historical buildings have survived, and many are now the property of either the Lincoln County Heritage Trust or the Museum of New Mexico. History buffs today enjoy walking the streets of Lincoln and exploring the old buildings. In these photographs, the old courthouse building is seen from behind. The hillside from which both photographs were made is now so overgrown with piñon and juniper trees that I was unable to get my shot precisely from J. R. Riddle's vantage point.

Trinity Site: Ground Zero, 1945

Early on the morning of July 16, 1945, the day after this photograph was made, the first atomic bomb was exploded from the platform atop this tower, a hundred feet above the desert floor of the Jornada del Muerto. Trinity Site, located on the Alamogordo Bombing and Gunnery Range, provided the isolation, secrecy, and safety required for the test. Still, the explosion broke windows as far as a hundred and twenty miles away. Hoping to hold the secret as long as possible, army officials simply said that there had been an accidental explosion at a munitions storage area.

Trinity Site Obelisk

Now a national historic landmark on the White Sands Missile Range, Trinity Site is open to visitors for only two days a year. These "open houses" are popular events, with hundreds of people making the long drive to see the site of this profound and history-altering event. In 1965, the army constructed a commemorative lava-stone obelisk precisely at Ground Zero. The blast crater has been backfilled, although a low structure preserves for visitors some of the green, glassy Trinitite—the explosion-fused desert sand. The blast's intense heat vaporized the steel tower, but the remains of one of its footings can still be seen, just left of the monument.

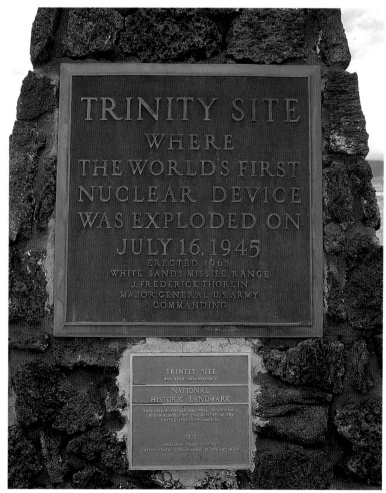

McDonald Ranch near Trinity Site, 1945

This photograph was taken in front of the McDonald ranch house, about two miles from Ground Zero, on the afternoon of July 13, 1945, a day and a half before the atomic bomb test explosion. The master bedroom of the ranch house, just out of view to the right, served as the bomb core's final assembly "clean room." Herb Lehr and Harry Daghlian are pictured here loading a small litter containing the bomb's completely assembled, plutonium-filled uranium capsule into the backseat of a U.S. government-issued 1942 Plymouth. The device was immediately—and very carefully, I imagine—driven the short distance to the blast tower for its final assembly into the bomb mechanism.

The adobe McDonald ranch house was built in 1913 by Franz Schmidt, a German immigrant who ran as many as twelve thousand sheep and a thousand cattle here on the eastern edge of the Jornada del Muerto. The ranch changed hands over the years and was acquired in the 1930s by George McDonald. In 1942, the Alamogordo Bombing and Gunnery Range took possession of much of the Jornada, including the McDonald land. This vast and remote area was initially used to train World War II bomber crews and later to test the atomic bomb. Other than shattering most of its windows, the blast from the explosion did not significantly damage the McDonald house. However, the elements did take their toll on the structure over the years, until finally, in 1982, the army stepped in to stabilize it. Two years later, the National Park Service restored the old ranch house to its pre-blast condition.

Roswell, circa 1900

The confluence of the Rio Hondo and the Pecos River was a favorite forage area for mid-nineteenth-century Texas cattlemen driving their herds northward. Located immediately west of the confluence, Roswell started with just a couple of adobe buildings, a store, and a small inn for travelers. The post office followed in 1873 and the town continued to grow, owing in part to the area's abundance of artesian water. Pictured here is a herd of cattle heading south along Roswell's Main Street, near the intersection with Second Street.

Roswell is New Mexico's fourth largest city today and is the primary business center for the southeastern part of the state. For much of the outside world, Roswell is famous for being central in UFO anecdotal history. The now-famous 1947 "Roswell Incident," which came to light in 1978, sparked considerable interest in UFOs and other unexplained phenomena. In response to this curiosity and the demand for information, the International UFO Museum and Research Center was incorporated in 1991, and for the past decade it has been one of Roswell's big tourist draws. I made my shot from the tallest stepladder I have ever climbed, with my tripod duct-taped to the top steps.

Bonito City, 1887

With the discovery of silver ore nearby, a small mining camp sprang to life in the early 1880s along the Rio Bonito, on the east flank of the Sierra Blanca. The camp grew quickly and was given the name Bonito City. Although modest in size, it could boast having most of the necessities of the time—a school, a post office, a general store, a saloon, a church, a hotel, and several residences. The Mayberry Hotel was the site of one of New Mexico's most bizarre and violent crimes. One night, when all were in bed, a young lodger began shooting and eventually killed several of the Mayberry family and other townspeople—seven fatalities in all—before he was finally shot and killed the next morning. His motive remains a mystery, but the story of that night's rampage is retold to this day as a fireside ghost story.

Bonito Lake

The ore in the Bonito City area played out, the miners moved on, and the post office finally closed up in 1911. Around this time, the Southern Pacific Railroad constructed a pipeline to bring water from the Rio Bonito to its trains traversing the dry desert lowlands around Carrizozo. In 1930, this water resource was enhanced with the construction of Bonito Dam, which formed Bonito Lake, whose waters flooded the old townsite. Alamogordo eventually obtained the water rights to Bonito Lake, and in 1957, a ninety-mile-long pipeline was built to supply water to the town and nearby Holloman Air Force Base. Today, Bonito Lake is a popular spot for camping and fishing.

In 1868, Captain Paul Dowlin built a water-powered mill near the Rio Ruidoso in the Sacramento Mountains. Dowlin had served in the Civil War's New Mexico Volunteers and later became the post trader at nearby Fort Stanton. A settlement developed near the mill and took on the name Dowlin's Mill, which would later be changed to Ruidoso. In his mill, Dowlin operated a bean thrasher, sawmill, and gristmill as well as a blacksmith shop and general store. Many notable figures reportedly spent time at the mill: Billy the Kid and Pat Garrett, John J. "Black Jack" Pershing and Douglas MacArthur, and Geronimo, to name a few.

The old mill in time fell into disrepair, but in 1944 Carmon and Leona Mae Phillips purchased and renovated the structure. They opened it as a gift shop in 1950, as Ruidoso was evolving toward the tourist center that it is today. The town's name has changed, and its former namesake Dowlin's Mill is now known as Ruidoso's Old Mill. Still operated by the Phillips family, the mill continues to offer tourists a variety of wares. Visitors can watch flour and cornmeal being ground on site, although the water that drives the big wheel today is recirculated by electric pump.

White Sands, 1945

White Sands National Monument

This beautiful image of pristine gypsum dune ripples at White Sands was made by Laura Gilpin, one of the preeminent photographers to work in New Mexico. Gilpin moved to Santa Fe following World War II, and during her very full career she photographed landscapes, still-lifes, and portraits, and is particularly well known for her images of the Pueblo and Navajo Indians. A few months before Gilpin photographed this scene, and about fifty miles to the north in the remote Jornada del Muerto, the U.S. Army exploded the first atomic bomb at Trinity Site.

Because sand dunes can migrate as much as forty feet in a year, and because Laura Gilpin made her photograph fifty-seven years before I ventured out onto the dunes to make mine, I knew that it would be impossible for me to find a dune arrangement identical to hers. However, I was able to use the profile of the San Andres Mountains, fifteen miles to the west, to help me frame a similar composition. I was also fortunate to find fresh, untracked ripples, the result of the preceding day's windstorm, much like those Gilpin recorded in her shot. The beauty and uniqueness of White Sands continues to attract photographers, artists, and other visitors from around the world.

Fraternal City Sanatorium, Alamogordo, circa 1910

Early in the twentieth century, many Southwestern towns were promoted as having an ideal climate to heal those afflicted with tuberculosis and other chronic lung problems. Following the arrival of the railroad in newly founded Alamogordo, a newspaper advertisement by the Alamogordo Improvement Company touted the area as "The Breathing Spot of the Southwest." Alamogordo businessmen invested in the Fraternal City Sanatorium, which opened for business in August, 1907, a few miles southeast of town at the base of the Sacramento Mountains. The facility was capable of housing a hundred and fifty, and rooms rented for seven dollars a week.

In February 1912, fire gutted the sanatorium's main building. Although all patients and staff were safely evacuated, the building was a total loss, and the facility never reopened. The few remaining signs of the complex are now mostly hidden by mesquite. The only historical familial connection that my wife, Carolyn, and I share with New Mexico involves her great-uncle, Loyd Lott of Georgia. Loyd suffered from tuberculosis; in 1908, he and his mother came to Alamogordo hoping the climate would facilitate his recovery. Although his health did temporarily improve in the desert air, he succumbed to the disease in 1910 and was buried in Alamogordo, not far from the sanatorium.

Alamogordo, early 1900s

Alamogordo owes its existence to the railroad. Charles and John Eddy, ranchers and land developers, were attracted by the idea of building a rail line from El Paso northward and eastward through New Mexico to connect with the great Midwestern lines. Their El Paso & Northeastern Railway was routed along the west side of the Sacramento Mountains, and in 1898, near an important spring in Alamo Canyon, the town of Alamogordo was born. Logging and ranching joined railroading as important area industries, and the town grew quickly. This view was shot from the corner of New York Avenue and Tenth Street, in the heart of downtown.

Most of these downtown Alamogordo buildings, including the onion-domed F. M. Avis block, have survived for the century that has passed between these photographs. The train still passes through Alamogordo, but the town's economic base has shifted away from the railroad to the military. Nearby Holloman Air Force Base has its roots in the bombing and gunnery training that took place there during World War II. This was one of those shots that I couldn't get from quite the spot I wanted—that would have involved setting up my large-format camera in the middle of this main intersection.

Cloudcroft, circa 1906

Cloudcroft sprang into existence with the construction of the Alamogordo & Sacramento Mountain Railway at the end of the nineteenth century. At first, it was simply a camp for rail workers, but it quickly evolved into a busy hub of activity. Summer visitors from the nearby desert lowlands were attracted by Cloudcroft's refreshingly cool mountain air, and loggers working the nearby timber frequented the town. This scene of Cloudcroft's main street—it's actually called Burro Street—caught my eye as I looked through old photographs of the area. I came up empty-handed in tracking down the story behind this scene, but nonetheless I decided to include it.

A couple of years after the historical photograph was taken, the entire block of downtown Cloudcroft buildings burned to the ground. At the far end of the street in both of these views, is the peaked roof of the old Texas Hotel. The hotel has survived for a full century and was for sale when I made my photograph. Pickup trucks and SUVs have replaced stock as the common mode of transportation here. The Cloudcroft area is still a popular tourist destination, although visitors have long been unable to travel here by rail.

Fresnal Canyon, Sacramento Mountains, 1920

Early travelers following the old road between the Tularosa Basin and the high country of the Sacramento Mountains around Cloudcroft saw this scene as they worked their way up the fossil-laden limestone escarpment via Fresnal Canyon. Barely visible are some of the route's guardrail posts about one-third of the way down on the right side of N. H. Darton's photograph. As early as 6000 B.C., hunter-gatherers of the Archaic culture lived in the Fresnal Shelter, a seasonal campsite beneath a rock overhang in the depths of Fresnal Canyon. Here archaeologists found a treasure trove of artifacts, including some of the earliest corn specimens found anywhere.

Today's US 82 through Fresnal Canyon runs roughly parallel to, and lower than, the old road. The highway's tunnel penetrates a limestone ridge for safer passage than the old route. Built in 1950, it is the only tunnel in the New Mexico highway system. Motorists today can park at the roadside pullout below the tunnel to enjoy the view of the canyon—or to chain up for slippery winter road conditions above. Accessing this camera station involved an exciting scramble, just up-canyon from a popular, technical rock-climbing area, up the steep slope from the highway to the old road above.

The first important liquid resource in Artesia's history was water. In the late nineteenth century, residents discovered that the area's groundwater, when tapped into, was so pressurized that it would supply artesian wells with abundant flow. Artesia and the surrounding country became an agricultural oasis, with seemingly unlimited, high-quality water for irrigation. This east-looking view of Artesia's main street was shot the year the town adopted its water-commemorating name, and two years before its official incorporation.

Oil was discovered in the Permian Basin in the 1920s, and the "black gold" quickly displaced water as Artesia's most valuable liquid resource. The oil and gas industry is still the major player in the area's economy, although farming and ranching are widespread as well. In a very successful public-private cooperative endeavor undertaken in 2001, seven blocks of Artesia's Main Street were transformed to a modern and attractive downtown. Some of the resulting improvements can be seen in this view, shot during a stormy winter sunset from the nose of one of the new roadway medians.

Flume at Eddy, 1890

Flume at Carlsbad

About the time Eddy (later renamed Carlsbad) was established in 1889, Charles Eddy and Pat Garrett partnered to form the Pecos Irrigation and Investment Company. By constructing a network of reservoirs, canals, and ditches along the Pecos River near the town, they hoped to provide water for the area's expanding agricultural and cattle industries. The wooden flume, shown here shortly after its completion and with its first flow, was one of the key elements of the water distribution system. It carried water from Lake Avalon across the Pecos River, whose natural channel passes below.

After twice being swept away by floods, the old wooden flume was replaced in 1903 by the concrete structure that is still in use today. At that time, the federal government took over operation of the irrigation system. When it was built, the new flume's support arches were the largest such concrete spans in the world. In the 1890 view, the countryside is barren and desiccated. In contrast, the background of today's scene, with its golf course and country-club homes, is decidedly more developed and lush. Most Pecos River flow has been impounded upriver or channeled outside of the original riverbed, so that little water now passes beneath the flume.

Carlsbad Caverns Natural Entrance, circa 1936

The discovery of Carlsbad Caverns is usually credited to Jim White, a cowboy who worked on the nearby XXX Ranch at the turn of the nineteenth and twentieth centuries. One sundown he spotted a dark, towering, funnel-shaped cloud that he at first thought to be a volcanic eruption but that turned out to be a massive swarm of bats. Picking his way through rocks and brush, he discovered that the bats were emerging from the ground through a large cliff-side opening that he would soon learn was the portal to a vast underground world. Known as the natural entrance, this entryway to the caverns is visible behind a cadre of Carlsbad Caverns National Park rangers.

Over the years, the phenomenon that Jim White witnessed—a mass exodus of bats from the depths of Carlsbad Caverns—has attracted visitors from around the world. During the summer months, hundreds of thousands of Mexican free-tail bats—and lesser numbers of several other bat varieties—crowd together on the ceiling of Bat Cave, located about 200 vertical feet below the natural entrance. At dusk, the bats emerge from the cave en masse and spend much of the night using their remarkable echolocation capability to catch insects, then return to the safety of the cave before dawn. On most summer evenings, onlookers congregate at this natural-entrance amphitheater to watch the bat flight, which had not yet begun when I made my photograph.

Carlsbad Caverns, 1907

Carlsbad Caverns National Park

The first documented exploratory ventures into Carlsbad Caverns took place in the early 1900s. Most of the early activity in the caverns involved mining (for fertilizer) of the prodigious accumulations of bat guano produced over the years by the hundreds of thousands of resident Mexican free-tail bats. This photograph, believed to be the first image of a cave formation, records a diorama-like scene of guano miners posed on the beautiful column and stalagmite at Devil's Spring. The man at top center is Charles Doss, owner of the guano mining operation. Note the explorer's pistol at the ready in the hand of the man beneath Doss.

My father and I ventured into Carlsbad Caverns by the natural-entrance route. After the initial descent into the darkness, and past the junction with Bat Cave, we continued down the trail until we came to Devil's Spring, several hundred feet below the surface. I made my photograph of the intricate formations and dark, spring-fed pool, illuminated only by the cave's electric lights. The caverns were protected in 1923 by the designation of a national monument, followed seven years later by the establishment of Carlsbad Caverns National Park. For good reasons, visitors are no longer allowed to touch the fragile formations, let alone climb on them for photo opportunities.

Southwestern New Mexico, it has been said, has a reality to match almost every stereotype of the American desert. Consider any symbol or image that means "desert" to most people, and the real thing has probably existed or still exists in this part of the Land of Enchantment.

Prickly pears and yuccas are here, of course, as well as roadrunners and coyotes. One might also recall, from a Hollywood version of the desert, tumbleweeds gusting down the street of a forlorn ghost town. In southwestern New Mexico that happens often, in Lake Valley, Shakespeare, and quite a few other abandoned places. Or there might come to mind a troop of cavalry riding from a lonely fort in pursuit of renegade Indians. That used to happen at Fort Selden and Fort Cummings. A gunfight in a frightened town? That was Elfego Baca's shootout at Frisco Plaza.

Many more images also reflect history: Mexican *bandidos* coming across the border to raid Columbus; vintage locomotives chuffing through rippling desert heat; pioneer families waylaid and massacred by Apaches; and even soiled doves plying their hearts of gold. And the New Mexico desert today still has grizzled prospectors, dusty bronc peelers, rattlesnakes, and Gila monsters, joined now by the eighteen-wheelers that roll down the interstate through the desert night.

Everything is here, that is, except saguaro cactus. Limited as the species is to southern Arizona and a sliver of California, this single, overly familiar symbol of the desert doesn't quite make it across the Arizona state line into New Mexico. Even so, with the notable exception of the saguaros, the realities of New Mexico's desert have become stereotypes and icons.

Consider for a moment, too, the Butterfield Overland Mail, which operated from 1857 to 1869. As a means of visualizing the desert environment, picture a Butterfield stagecoach jarring and swaying across southwestern New Mexico, pulled by a six-horse team, crossing arid plains and dry washes, then winding to the foot of desert mountains where a way station stands near a sweet water spring.

That was the reality of Cookes Spring at the base of Cookes Peak and of similar places at Soldiers Farewell and Steins Peak. The flats traversed by the stage are the basins of the Basin and Range country, sprinkled with mesquite and alkali barrens; the mountains

SOUTHWESTERN BASIN AND RANGE COUNTRY

Main Street, Las Cruces, Early 1900s. Photograph by W.T. Lee

are the ranges between the basins, all aligned in parallel rows. These mountains stand as rock sentinels, or islands in the sky. Only the highest of them are clothed in summit forests; most of the ranges instead are studded with shrubby live oak, cacti of various species, and clumps of beargrass and sotol—all plants that were used for various purposes by the Apaches in times past.

Yet one superb nondesert area must be mentioned in any account of southwestern New Mexico's landscape. Differing from all the rest, it is the Mogollon Mountains–Black Range country, generally known as the Gila since it contains the headwaters of the Gila River. The mountains of this fifty-by-hundred-mile area rise more than ten thousand feet, and forests of ponderosa pine go on and on. Everything is the eroded remnant of an old volcanic highland, with canyons and creeks running down the sides in crazy-quilt branchings. Some eight hundred and seventy square miles here are designated as the Gila Wilderness—America's first officially designated wilderness. It is remarkable that after centuries of human presence in New Mexico, here is an area that has continued so little known and so little disturbed by man.

≈   ≈   ≈   ≈

Time and circumstances have not been kind to small communities in New Mexico, and perhaps especially not to those in the southwestern part of the state. A few communities here, Silver City for one, have grown somewhat in modern times. Another, Las Cruces, has grown surprisingly, with a current population of seventy thousand. But other small towns have shrunk, have become poorer, and have known daily struggles for a bit of vitality. Some have disappeared.

Bill Stone's old and new photographs bear this out. For one thing, Bill has rephotographed several old mining communities that over the years have become ghost towns, or almost: Kelly, Chloride, Hillsboro, and Lake Valley. Santa Rita is a special example: It became a town when its nearby copper mines were underground, but the mines became an open-pit operation and eventually swallowed up the place where the town had been.

Other photo pairs again reveal how the works of man have persisted—or not. Many of the "then" photos have a direct, open look about them, and the photographers of past times certainly approached their subjects with enthusiasm. In their photographs are buildings, streets, throngs of people, even entire communities, all bustling with the life and times of New Mexico.

As these photos are viewed a century or so later, however, some of them look nothing but old—sometimes quaintly old, occasionally grotesquely old. And as ever, the contrasts are revealed in Bill's present-day pictures. In several "now" photos we see that some mine or building or community of the older photo has been abandoned or demolished.

As for the reasons why? "Outworn by time or events," we might generalize, suspecting that reasons are complex and intertwined. An occasional mining town may now be a ghost, it is true, because the ore simply ran out. And most army forts of New Mexico were abandoned for a single reason—the Indian dangers lessened. But in other cases it is likely that several causes contributed to decline. For mines and mining towns, changing times brought competition, increased costs, decreased prices for what was produced, machinery obsolescence, declining yields—things that can pull the economics of a mine right out from under it. At Lake Valley, though, causes of decline were dramatic: A catastrophic fire in the town, together with 1893's utter collapse of the silver market, largely did in the place.

Finally, and more recently, the advent of automobiles and good roads meant that, in many towns, people were no longer so tied to their small communities.

Yet some of Bill's photos do show manmade things that have endured through years of changing times. The Luna County courthouse at Deming is an example (see p. 138); it is a lesson in longevity and historic preservation.

Historians have called the 1880s in the western United States the age of the cattle barons, on account of the explosive growth in ranching that followed the Civil War. The Diamond A Ranch, originally established by Michael Gray and located in southwestern New Mexico, was one of the huge ranching outfits that developed during this time. It eventually became one of the largest cattle operations in American history, with ranchland extending from the Mexican border in the Bootheel all the way to Silver City and Lake Valley, and with even more land farther north along the Rio Grande. The grasslands in the Animas Valley and the country around the Animas Mountains, shown here, were always the focal point of the ranch.

By the 1960s, a boom in western ranchland resulted in property being sold at prices that were several times their sustainable cattle-yield value. The massive Diamond A Ranch was doomed, and large portions were sold off. What remained in the Bootheel became known as the Gray Ranch and was eventually acquired by the Nature Conservancy in an effort to preserve what the organization felt to be one of "earth's last great places." The Animas Foundation bought the Gray Ranch in 1994 and is operating it in an environmentally responsible fashion, with a ranchland ethic that should serve as a model for years to come. Notice the change in the foreground drainage, probably due to the highway, which is just out of view. Nearby, I noticed a "Running Water" highway warning sign, which someone had modified with the plea, "Pray For…," written in magic marker.

International Boundary Monument No. 40, 1892

International Boundary Monument No. 40 is one of a series of markers delineating the U.S.-Mexico boundary, as established by the Gadsden Purchase of 1853 and surveyed by Major William H. Emory. Built in 1855 of cut stone and standing more than twelve feet tall, the monument marks the boundary's turning point at the northeastern corner of New Mexico's Bootheel. However, a subsequent resurvey of the boundary revealed that, as originally constructed, this monument had been placed a mile too far eastward. In this 1892 view by photographer D. R. Payne of Albuquerque, the government crew is finishing the reconstruction of the monument in its proper location, using the original stone blocks.

Aside from the range and border fences that now appear in the scene, very little has changed. The extreme remoteness of the borderlands struck me as I imagine it did the early surveyors and photographer working in the area. The pre-dawn solitude was palpable as I set off alone by flashlight from my car camp to walk the three miles for this photograph. I arrived just as the sun's first rays lit up the monument. Later in the morning and back on the remote dirt approach road, I met four brothers from nearby Deming prospecting a family claim for silver, hoping to realize their deceased father's long-held dream of striking it rich.

Columbus, 1916

In the pre-dawn hours of March 9, 1916, a group of several hundred insurgents, led by Mexican revolutionary Pancho Villa, attacked the sleepy little border town of Columbus. The Villistas looted and burned many of the town's businesses and buildings. They also sacked some of nearby Camp Furlong, a U.S. Army installation whose soldiers performed border-patrol duty. By the time the soldiers and civilians of Columbus were able to drive the Villistas away, eighteen Americans and perhaps as many as two hundred of the Mexican bandits lay dead. This view of the town, taken from a water tower, shows some of the destruction inflicted during the raid.

Pancho Villa's raid on Columbus was, until the tragic events of September 11, 2001, the only foreign attack suffered by the United States on its contiguous territory since the War of 1812. With Camp Furlong serving as the support depot for the Punitive Expedition into Mexico to catch Villa, the combined military and civilian population of Columbus swelled to eleven thousand, making it the biggest city in New Mexico for a time. Today, about two thousand people—including many retirees, artists, and small-town aficionados—call Columbus home. With a threefold population increase since 1990, Columbus is the second-fastest-growing city in the state. I was unable to climb a water tower for my photo, so I settled with this view taken from the top of Cootes Hill, in what is now Pancho Villa State Park (the name of which, oddly, would seem to commemorate the villain).

Following Pancho Villa's raid, several dozen American troopers chased the Villistas out of Columbus and pursued them a short distance into Mexico. A week later, General John J. "Black Jack" Pershing led the Punitive Expedition, consisting of several thousand troops and lasting nearly a year, deep into Mexico to apprehend Villa. In this scene, photographed a short time after the raid, soldiers of the U.S. Army's Signal Corps are flag-signaling from the top of Camp Furlong's Cootes Hill to another signal party located in Mexico. The flag message no doubt had some bearing on the hunt for Villa.

Although Villa was never caught, the Punitive Expedition helped prepare U.S. troops for World War I. It was the first time that airplanes and motorized vehicles were deployed in a combat scenario. Richard Dean, seen here on Cootes Hill, is the great-grandson of James T. Dean, a Columbus grocer killed during the attack when, unaware that the town was under siege, he ran out to help extinguish the Commercial Hotel fire, set by the Villistas. Richard is looking out over Columbus, where he and his wife, Betty, have lived since retiring to the area. The Deans play a key role in the preservation of Columbus' important history.

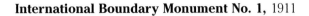

This international scene includes Mexico in the foreground, New Mexico Territory in the left middle ground, and the Franklin Mountains of Texas in the background. The Rio Grande flows beneath the large railroad trestle and off the right edge of the view. Just left of and below the center of the image, enclosed by a fence, is International Boundary Monument No. 1, the initial point of the U.S.-Mexico boundary line that extends from the Rio Grande westward to the Pacific Ocean. The encampment to the right of the monument is the temporary headquarters of Francisco Madero, a leader of the Mexican Revolution, who ousted the long-standing dictator Porfirio Diaz in May, 1911, the same month the photograph was taken. This border-hugging location offered a number of advantages to Madero and his supporters during the political unrest and uncertainty of the Revolution.

A few months after the historical photograph was taken, Francisco Madero assumed office as Mexico's president, a position he held for only a short time before being assassinated during a coup that led to the 1917 reformation of Mexico's constitution. This scene today is dominated by extraction industries, including brick factories and the prominent but temporarily closed American Smelting and Refining Company's copper facility, which dates from 1887. The dark shadow is cast by Mount Cristo Rey, famous for its summit cross, the destination of Easter pilgrimages. I felt more secure during my climb up the steep slope of the mountain into Mexico to make my shot knowing that a U.S. Border Patrol officer was watching me from his vehicle, parked at the far left and mostly hidden by the shadow.

Dripping Springs, circa 1906

Eugene Van Patten, a New York native, worked for the Butterfield Overland Mail Company and fought for the Confederacy in the Civil War. He was involved in the pivotal Battle of Glorieta Pass in which Union forces defeated the advancing Fifth Texas Regiment and prevented the Confederates from taking control of the Colorado gold fields. In the 1870s, he built Van Patten's Mountain Camp near Dripping Springs, on the west slope of the Organ Mountains. The camp, which boasted some sixteen guest rooms, a large dining room, and a concert hall, proved to be very popular around the turn of the century. Camp guests included notables such as Pat Garrett and Pancho Villa.

Financial problems befell Van Patten, and in 1917 he sold his camp to Dr. Nathan Boyd, a physician from San Francisco. Boyd's wife contracted tuberculosis and he converted the resort, now named Dripping Springs, into a sanatorium. Over the years, Dripping Springs changed hands a couple more times before it and the nearby Cox Ranch were acquired by the Nature Conservancy. The Conservancy then transferred ownership to the Bureau of Land Management, which now administers the site to preserve the cultural history and unique natural environment of the area.

Las Cruces, early 1900s

MAIN STREET, LAS CRUCES, NEW MEXICO.

Las Cruces' Main Street in the early 1900s was a busy place. In this view, a mixture of horse-drawn buggies, wagons, and early-vintage automobiles lines the dusty thorough-fare. Las Cruces was founded in 1849 when residents of the crowded nearby town of Doña Ana were offered free land if they would help establish a new settlement. The railroad arrived in 1881 and forever changed the economic and societal nature of the area. Within six months, the county seat and many important government offices were transferred from nearby Mesilla to Las Cruces.

Las Cruces is now New Mexico's second largest city. During the nation's widespread urban renewal era of the 1960s and '70s, a third of the historic buildings in the downtown area were razed, and many others were moved or refurbished. In an effort to revitalize Las Cruces' urban center, a few blocks of old Main Street were replaced with a bricked pedestrian mall, closed to vehicular traffic. However, the rebirth of downtown never materialized the way civic leaders had hoped, and now once again, thirty-some years later, there is discussion of a new revitalization effort.

Modoc Mine, 1904

Situated high on the western flank of the Organ Mountains, the Modoc Mine yielded considerable lead and silver during its half-century of periodic operation. In 1898, the Modoc Mining Company invested the sizable sum of $1 million in developing the infrastructure for a state-of-the-art operation—deep shafts, a three-quarter-mile gravity-powered ore tram, steam-powered processing equipment, and a four-hundred-and-twenty-foot-deep water well. The tall building left of center in this view is the six-story ore concentrating mill and the lower terminus of the ore tram. Piles of firewood, cut in the mountains and bought from local laborers for one dollar per mule-load, are stacked around the base of the smokestacks.

The Modoc Mine's ore was depleted in 1907, and in the 1920s the mine's structures were sold for scrap. Still faintly visible are the hillside platform excavated for the concentrating mill and the scars from some of the mineshafts upslope from the mill. The piles of firewood are long gone and the tenacious desert vegetation has reclaimed most of the former building sites. While waiting several hours for the Organs to emerge from storm clouds, I walked into this scene along the hiking trail that is visible in the photograph. I found a few vestiges of the mill's foundation and the boulder-choked well.

Lake Valley, circa 1890

Lake Valley came to life with the 1882 discovery of the Bridal Chamber silver deposit in a nearby mine. In eleven years, more than two and a half million ounces of silver were harvested. Lake Valley's population swelled to four thousand, and businesses flourished as miners and service trade people moved to town. The railroad arrived in 1884, and a spur line was built directly into the Bridal Chamber so that solid silver could be loaded right onto the railcars; much of it was so pure that it required no smelting. Henry A. Schmidt's photograph records a wonderful moment, with a train on final approach to Lake Valley, chugging along beneath Monument Peak.

Lake Valley suffered a devastating blow in 1893 when silver was devalued. Just two years later, disaster struck again when most of Main Street burned to the ground. From 1920 to 1950, Lake Valley experienced occasional episodes of activity with the commercial mining of manganese ore. Finally, in 1994, the last full-time residents moved away. Very few buildings have survived, and the place is peacefully quiet today. The Lake Valley area has for many years been well known to paleontologists for the large number of unique marine fossils found in the rocks.

Fort Selden, 1867

Construction at Fort Selden began in 1865 on the east bank of the Rio Grande, near the southern end of the Jornada del Muerto. The fort's primary roles were to protect the settlers of nearby Mesilla Valley and to guard travelers and livestock traversing the Jornada del Muerto. It was newly completed when Nicholas Brown shot this photograph from the rooftop of the post trader's store. The officers' compound and quarters are the structures in the foreground, and the prison and top-floor courtroom comprise the two-story structure left of center. A heliograph signaling station was located atop Lookout Mountain, in the background.

Fort Selden State Monument

Fort Selden was fully abandoned in 1891, a short twenty-five years after its establishment. Around this time, New Mexico's Fort Union, Fort Marcy, and Fort Cummings were also closed, along with two dozen other posts throughout the West. Threats to the settlement of the West had substantially subsided, and the military felt it could operate more effectively from a smaller number of better-configured facilities. A contractor was allowed to salvage Fort Selden's doors, windows, and hardware in payment for his work to remove the bodies from the post cemetery. For more than a hundred years, the old adobe walls have been slowly melting back to the earth. Fort Selden is now a state monument.

The Giants of the Mimbres, 1867

The Giants of the Mimbres is a collection of pinnacles, columns, boulders, and mushroom and balanced rocks situated in a small valley near the west bank of the Mimbres River. Created by a combination of erosion and tectonic block uplift of volcanic tuff, the Giants stand just a few miles from the geologically related and better-known City of Rocks. U.S. Boundary Commissioner John R. Bartlett described and named the Giants in 1851. In 1867, English physician and photographer William A. Bell explored and photographed the Giants while working on a survey of the thirty-second parallel for the Kansas Pacific Railroad. Note the person on the boulder and the wagon at the far right.

Some of the same woody plants can be identified in these scenes, although there are more prickly pear cactus and fewer grasses today than in Bell's time. One stormy summer evening, as I waited at the Giants for the light to develop, a dramatic, black-sky monsoonal storm cell—with torrential rain—passed just to the east. I waited out the storm under an overhanging boulder. Within minutes after the storm's passage, I could hear water churning through the usually dry channel of the Mimbres River, nearly a half-mile away. By the time I returned to my vehicle, the pulse of runoff had passed and the channel was quickly returning to its pre-deluge condition.

Luna County Courthouse, Deming, circa 1910

This photograph of the Luna County Courthouse in Deming was apparently made shortly after the building was completed in 1910. This landmark building's style—including the Greek portico and tall clock tower—is similar to that of many nineteenth-century public buildings throughout the Midwest. It's hard to say exactly what the occasion was that is recorded here. The scene has an interesting mixture of the formality of the group posed on the steps and the casual nature of the boys hanging off the light pole and the man with his bicycle.

The jail was built just to the left (east) of the courthouse in 1918. Now an annex to the main building, the old jail is an example of the Prairie-style architecture that was popularized by Frank Lloyd Wright. The trials of several of Pancho Villa's Villistas who were involved in the 1916 raid on Columbus were held here in the courthouse. The landscaping has filled in nicely over the years. The lightpoles are gone but a flagpole and memorial to a local casualty of World War I have been added to the scene. Festivities of Deming's annual Great American Duck Races take place in the park to the right of the courthouse.

Fort Cummings, circa 1888

Located a few miles southeast of Cookes Peak, Fort Cummings was established in 1863 at Cookes Spring, an abundant and important water source for the region. A few years before the fort was built, the Butterfield Overland Mail Company established one of its stations near the spring. The fort's primary function was to protect travelers, freight haulers, and mail carriers passing through the area, often on the Butterfield Trail, from attacks by Apache Indians. Fort Cummings was abandoned in 1873 but was reactivated for a while in 1880 and again in 1886, on both occasions to help with Apache conflicts.

Fort Cummings was closed for the last time around 1891, and over the past hundred and twelve years, all of the buildings, mostly built of adobe, have almost completely melted back to the earth. These photographs were made from a rocky ridge that affords a fine overview of the fort's site, as well as part of Cookes Range, on the left, and the distant Mimbres Mountains. I was excited to find the exact foreground rocks to match my view with J. R. Riddle's image of long ago. Fort Cummings today feels extremely remote and isolated, much as it most certainly did to the nineteenth-century soldiers stationed there.

Chloride, 1893

Nestled along Chloride Creek in the western foothills of the Black Range, the town of Chloride owes its existence to a muleskinner named Harry Pye, who in the 1870s discovered silver ore nearby as he was hauling freight for the U.S. Army. Once this news spread, a tent city quickly sprang up, and by 1881 Chloride was a bustling place replete with most basic small-town amenities. This photograph was taken by Henry Schmidt, a brilliant German immigrant who served as Chloride's assayer and surveyor. He was also a talented photographer who left behind many fine images, including several depicting territorial New Mexico mining towns.

In a scenario experienced by many western mining towns, Chloride's boom was rather short-lived. The decline started in the mid-1890s, when gold was selected as the nation's monetary standard. Silver value plummeted so low that the hard work of mining was no longer worth the effort. By 1900 most of the miners had moved on, and Chloride became the quiet little mountain town that it still is today, a century later. Several buildings have survived through the years and can be identified in both views, as can the "hanging tree," which still stands in the middle of the main street.

Founded in 1877 following the discovery of gold in the nearby mountains, Hillsboro quickly thrived and eventually boasted a population of more than twelve hundred. The town's growth garnered it the seat of Sierra County, and in 1892 a courthouse, considered by some "the most stately building in New Mexico," was built. It appears in the right background of this scene. One of New Mexico's most celebrated trials was held here—that of the accused murderers of Judge Albert Fountain and his son, who were apparently killed because of Fountain's investigation into the Lincoln County War. The accused were acquitted of the crime, and to this day the case remains unsolved.

The courthouse's remains are barely visible in my photograph. The building was mostly dismantled following the county seat's 1938 relocation to Hot Springs (renamed Truth or Consequences in 1951). Hillsboro's present population, which includes a contingent of artists, writers, and others attracted by small-town life, is just a fraction of what it was during its heyday. It's difficult to see through the dense tree cover today, but several Hillsboro buildings have survived the century that has passed between these photographs.

Elephant Butte, 1911

Water from the Rio Grande has been used for irrigation since at least A.D. 1000, when Indians living in the valley built a canal system to water their crops. Over the years, extreme variations in flow—from raging floods to extended droughts—challenged even the most resourceful farmers. Along with increased settlement of the Rio Grande Valley in the 1800s came an interest in damming the river to provide more reliable irrigation. Construction of the Elephant Butte Dam by the U.S. Bureau of Reclamation involved a contingent of some nine hundred workers, many of whom lived in the tent city shown here early in the project.

Elephant Butte Dam was completed in 1916, with a price tag of more than $5 million. Engineers used concrete-encased sandstone blocks to build the three-hundred-foot tall, third-of-a-mile-long structure. Once the dam was completed and the lake basin filled, Elephant Butte Lake became, at the time, the world's largest manmade body of water, with two hundred miles of shoreline. This view is looking across the Damsite Marina complex to Elephant Butte (an ancient volcanic cone), and on northward to the distant Fra Cristobal Range, which didn't record on the 1911 image because of the old film's response to distant haze.

Santa Rita Mine, circa 1915

Discovered in 1798, the Santa Rita Mine has been an important source of copper for two centuries. By the early 1800s, a wealthy Mexican merchant, Francisco Elguea, had established a formidable mining operation, which led to the birth of the town of Santa Rita, seen in this photograph. By 1910, most of the high-grade ore had played out, and mining operations switched to the extraction of low-grade ore, dug from the surface. Surface mining employed huge steam-operated shovels, a few of which are at work and generating smoke and dust in the background of this scene. Notice the family laundry hanging out to dry on the clothesline.

Over the years, the big shovels continued to dig, the Santa Rita pit grew, and the town was forced to move out of harm's way several times. Eventually, there was no place left for Santa Rita to go, and it was completely swallowed up by what would become one of the world's largest open-pit mines, now owned by the massive Phelps Dodge Corporation. Today the hole is about a mile across and more than a third of a mile deep. For scale, note a few of the mammoth ore trucks down in the pit. Today's prevailing economic and market conditions have rendered uncertain all future operations at the Santa Rita Mine. The region's prosperity is tied to the boom and bust cycles of the mining industry.

Silver City, 1902

Following the discovery of silver nearby, the town of Silver City was established in 1870. It quickly grew and within a year became the seat of Grant County. Woodcutting and overgrazing eventually stripped the surrounding hills of their natural vegetation, and runoff from heavy rains became a recurring problem. In 1895, a dramatic flood scoured Main Street into an arroyo. On August 24, 1902, shortly before this photograph was taken, another flood washed away what was left of Main Street. The resulting gully, visible here littered with uprooted trees and debris, split Silver City in half. The railroad depot can be seen on the far bank.

In the early 1900s, numerous floods roared through Silver City's Big Ditch, as the Main Street watercourse came to be known—a name borrowed from the Panama Canal that was being constructed at the time. Slowly, land conservation and drainage stabilization efforts were implemented, and in 1936 the Civilian Conservation Corps lined much of the ditch with masonry. In 1980, Silver City dedicated the Big Ditch as a downtown park. Today's visitors can enjoy the park's walking paths, bridges, stairways, and benches. The Warren House, seen at the upper right, is one of the few old Main Street buildings that has survived to this day.

This photograph of the western flank of the Mogollon Mountains was made by A. B. Searle, a geologist for the U.S. Geological Survey. The view shows the eroded bluffs where the terrain transitions from the lowlands of the San Francisco River to the forested mountain highlands in the distance. The same year Searle recorded this scene, Aldo Leopold received his forestry degree from Yale University and began working in New Mexico and Arizona, both still territories at the time, for the four-year-old U.S. Forest Service.

Gila Wilderness

By 1912, when New Mexico became a state, Aldo Leopold had been promoted to supervisor of northern New Mexico's Carson National Forest. Earlier he had worked in the forestlands of southwestern New Mexico, where he began formulating a responsible and ethical approach to wildlife and game management. Leopold had a vision of wildland preservation that involved setting aside and protecting from man's impact large tracts of undeveloped land. Thanks to Leopold's forward-looking conservation philosophy, the Forest Service in 1924 established the world's first wilderness area, the Gila Wilderness—a small part of which is seen here. Today's vitally important wilderness preservation effort across the country—and in other parts of the world—owes its existence to the important work spearheaded by Aldo Leopold here in New Mexico three-quarters of a century ago.

Kelly, circa 1885

Situated on the north flank of the Magdalena Mountains, the mining town of Kelly at one time boasted a population of about three thousand. The town owed its existence to the lead, zinc, silver, copper, and gold that miners found in the nearby mountains. With the discovery of smithsonite, an important component of paint pigment, the Sherwin-Williams Paint Company purchased a large mine here in the early 1900s. Socorro photographer Joseph Smith recorded this scene of a gathering of locals on Kelly's main street. The background hillsides bear evidence of mining activity.

The shadows I found on Kelly's main street were cast by piñon and juniper trees rather than by boomtown buildings, as in the old photo. The town has all but disappeared in the years since the mines played out. The post office finally closed in the 1940s. A small church building, a cemetery, a few vestigial foundations, and some relic mining structures are about all of Kelly that remains today.

Socorro, circa 1883

For centuries prior to the Spaniards' arrival in New Mexico, Piro Indians occupied several pueblos in the middle Rio Grande Valley. In 1626, Spanish colonizers established the mission of Nuestra Señora de Socorro (Our Lady of Aid) at the pueblo of Pilabó. During the 1680 Pueblo Revolt, however, the mission and pueblo were burned and abandoned. The site remained uninhabited for over a century until around 1815, when Socorro was resettled. The village grew slowly under Spanish and Mexican rule and during early territorial days until the August 1880 arrival of the railroad. By the end of that year, the population had grown to nearly twenty-five hundred and Socorro was entering an economic boom. Socorro's plaza, busy with a Fourth of July parade, is seen in this view shot from the second story of a prominent downtown building.

I obtained permission to make my shot from what I believe is the same second floor window that was used a hundred and twenty years ago to photograph the holiday parade. For a few decades in the latter nineteenth century, Socorro was the center of one of the country's most productive mining districts. This heritage is reflected by the presence of both the New Mexico Institute of Mining and Technology, which opened here in 1893, and the New Mexico Bureau of Geology and Mineral Resources. Socorro was unable to maintain the boom that came with the railroad and the mines in the late nineteenth century, but it has nonetheless continued to play an important role in New Mexico's story.

Magdalena Stock Shipping Pens, 1885

In 1880, New Mexico cattle numbered about a hundred and thirty-seven thousand head; by 1889, that number had grown tenfold. Much of this growth was due to the coming of the railroad. Following the 1885 completion of the Atchison, Topeka & Santa Fe Railway's branch to Magdalena, stockmen developed an open-range route along which they drove their herds of sheep and cattle eastward to Magdalena. Known as the Magdalena Stock Driveway, this corridor, together with the railroad, provided access to the outside market for ranchers throughout much of west-central New Mexico and eastern Arizona. Located alongside the tracks, these shipping pens held the stock until they were sent off by rail.

Concerns that the Magdalena Stock Driveway might be blocked by the area's developing homesteads prompted cattlemen to petition the federal government to set aside a formalized route, thereby guaranteeing their access to Magdalena. This request was approved, and a Roosevelt-era Civilian Conservation Corps project constructed two hundred miles of range fence around the five-to-ten-mile-wide corridor. The CCC also drilled water wells about every ten miles. But the stock pens have now been quiet for more than thirty years. Trucking supplanted cattle drives and the railroad as the preferred means of transporting herds to market, and the Magdalena branch of the railroad was abandoned in 1972.

A Visit to Winston and Chloride

We were headed west on State Road 52, a stretch of old pavement that connects Winston and Chloride to the rest of the world. These little southwestern New Mexico towns are nestled in the hilly skirts of the Black Range, in one of the more remote parts of the state. On either side of us as the road gradually ascended, the creosote-bush desert gave way to thin grasses and scattered junipers: rangeland, but rangeland where cattle have to scrounge for every bite.

Three of us had set out that spring morning, Bill Stone, writer Bob Julyan, and me, and our purpose for the day was to check out five or six old photos that Bill thought might be suitable for rephotography. Bill was driving while Bob and I browsed the pictures.

"Not many *typical* towns in New Mexico," Bob said, his thought sparked by the photos. "Not many Maple Streets, picket fences, or tidy lawns—that kind of thing."

"You're probably right," Bill said. "There're all kinds of towns, but between not having enough water and—"

Just then a Volvo sedan passed us from behind, one of only a few vehicles on the road that morning. As it pulled ahead Bob squinted and said, "Look, that car's full of clowns!" And indeed, through the back window of the Volvo we caught glimpses of red wigs, flouncy collars, balloons, and greasepaint.

A few minutes later we arrived at Winston and learned the reason for the clowns—the annual Winston-Chloride Spring Fiesta was getting under way. The Volvo and other cars and pickups were parked across from the town's one little store, in front of which the five clowns were preparing for their act and chatting with people. Members of the Ladies' Clown Club of Truth or Consequences, they had come to participate in the fiesta parade. It was our luck to hit upon the celebration, and we were just in time for the parade.

The procession went down the one paved street and up the only other street. It consisted of two or three shiny sports cars and a sporty pickup, the horses and riders of the Sierra County Mounted Patrol and the mounted patrols of one or two other counties, the clown ladies walking with floppy shoes and throwing hard candies to the spectators, a vintage Forest Service pickup with a Smokey Bear impersonator and a pretty girl waving from the back, and a flatbed truck partially decorated as a float. It was a great parade!

NEW MEXICO REFLECTIONS

San Vicente Arroyo, South of Silver City, 1910

After visiting with the crowd at the town's picnic pavilion, we set out to find the spot from which our old photo of Winston had been taken. Turning in at a weedy lane past an abandoned house, we stopped and hiked up a grassy ridge. But as we looked back, we could see that a "now" photo wasn't going to work. In the hundred years since the old photo had been made, the near end of the town had crumbled and vanished. Elsewhere only one house was still recognizable, and trees obscured all the rest.

Five miles farther on, at Chloride, we had better luck. Originally a silver mining town, Chloride has been for decades nearly a ghost town. Our historical photo looked down from a canyonside viewpoint, and it was easy enough to find the same spot and match up several existing buildings with those in the old photo. A large live oak tree grew in the very middle of the only street, exactly where it appeared in the picture of a century earlier.

We had two or three more successes with old photos of nearby places, such as the canyon leading to the three-house village of Chise, and as we drove home that evening, our conversation returned to New Mexico's communities. Between us we were familiar with most of them: Farmington, Raton, Las Vegas, Gallup, Española, Santa Rosa, Tucumcari, Clovis, Portales, Socorro, Silver City, Truth or Consequences, Roswell, Carlsbad, Las Cruces, Alamogordo, Deming, Hobbs. Every town has a different and distinct character.

Each town or small city also owes its existence to some unique circumstance, be it mining, railroading, logging, the oil patch, irrigation, dry farming, dry climate (once a necessity of health resorts), or mountain climate (still a necessity for recreation resorts). A few of these communities had originated as Spanish Colonial villages.

The little mountain city of Los Alamos was the home of the atomic bomb. I wondered aloud and doubtfully whether any other state might have such diverse communities. Or as Bob had said, so few that had the look of what people imagine to be typical American small towns.

Capturing Change

Rephotography is a concept rooted in the realism of photographs and the nearly instantaneous action of cameras. In photography's early days, that which most impressed people was the amazing realism of photographic images, not any artistic qualities they had. Photos were in a different realm than the pictures of painters—their realism was so much greater, and they were made in short, real moments of time. Accordingly, the notion of faithfully capturing change, by photographing a particular scene or object once and then again later from exactly the same spot, had to have occurred to photographers early on.

How obvious that idea now seems, yet it was a door opened only incidentally by the medium of photography. Here was a means for seeing and perhaps even measuring changes that might be caused by the passage of time or by human agency in landforms, landscapes, and street scenes. By rephotography, things could be seen not only as they were, but also as they became. Over the last century or so, rephotography has in fact chiefly served as a valuable tool in various scientific applications. In this book, of course, the objective is more on the side of human history and landscape aesthetics.

It is surprising how many unfamiliar, now-forgotten places and things are pictured in the "then" photos of this book: old mines, forts, buildings, and scenic vistas. Bill Stone's emphasis, however, is on natural landscapes—few, if any, of which are unaffected by human activities, even in such a thinly populated state as New Mexico. Many of the landscapes here could be termed more precisely "naturalistic." But Bill's penchant is for scenes that reflect the powers of nature and spur greater understanding of such powers. The book is a celebration of such scenes and places.

An Ongoing Inspiration

Among those who entered New Mexico after it came under the control of the United States in 1846 were a number of photographers.

Some came to stay; others merely passed through as members of exploring expeditions, recording the natural and manmade landscapes they found. As we have seen in these pages, their landscape photography ranged from mere "record shots" to wonderfully composed and expressive photos.

Even more indelible and accomplished were the images of photographers who worked in New Mexico in the 1920s and middle years of the twentieth century—Paul Strand, Edward Weston, Ansel Adams, Laura Gilpin, and others. These were the modernists of American photography, who made of the medium a truly expressive art form.

Without exception, both the early-day photographers and the modernists found New Mexico different from anything they had known. But they were intrigued. Here was a strange land, sometimes stark and arid, but beautiful for those who could appreciate it. Here were Pueblo, Navajo, and Apache Indians, most of them following ancestral ways of life. Here, too, were the descendants of the *conquistadores*. These longtime New Mexicans were resourceful people, leading traditional lives in Santa Fe and Albuquerque and other towns and villages, some of which were particularly photogenic.

After statehood arrived in 1912, New Mexico became attractive not only for photographers but for artists, writers, poets, and folklorists—how numerous they became!—all enthralled by the same things that the photographers had already found. Aided by their artistic interpretations, New Mexico became even more pointedly a land of myth, spirit, and romance. Here were sensed interactions between the people and the land that were not seen, or had been lost, elsewhere. Part of the difference here was a palpable sense of time or, as some said, of timelessness. Not only historians but anyone could glimpse the long passage of time in New Mexico and actually feel what one writer called "the power and pathos of time." Another difference was the light. Not only photographers and painters but anyone could sense the sun's brightness and the air's clarity, and marvel at the ethereal blue of the skies of New Mexico.

Even now, affinities grow every day in New Mexico between people and the land. That is what this book is about, what it is for. The photos on these pages are meant to intrigue and inspire. Surely the past and the present will become more clear, as we see what was and what now is, and ponder the differences.

Leopold's Legacy

The concept of preserving wilderness, as almost every enthusiast of wild places knows, is deeply rooted in New Mexico. Back in the 1920s, it was largely in the mind of Aldo Leopold, and by his efforts, that the wilderness idea began and became reality—the idea of saving at least those few wild places that remained free of human domination.

Leopold came as a young ranger to the Apache National Forest in 1909, equipped with both academic training and an outdoorsman's interest in wildlife and hunting. In those days, killing wolves, bears, and mountain lions was part of a forest ranger's job—making the forest safe for huntable game, as well as for people and their livestock. In time, though, Leopold began to question the wisdom of such policy. His thoughts continued evolving as he moved to northern New Mexico to become a supervisor of the Carson National Forest. He later worked in the Forest Service's regional office in Albuquerque, where he met others concerned about the dwindling of the West's wild lands and wildlife. With the supervisor of the Gila National Forest, he drew the boundaries of the area that he proposed to "set aside" as wilderness.

As a result of his leadership, the Gila Wilderness, more than a half-million acres, was indeed formally designated by order of the Secretary of Agriculture in 1924. The designation covered that part of the Gila National Forest that had no roads or human habitation, and it was the first national-forest wilderness, an unspoiled place wherein the processes of nature would reign.

In the same year that the Gila Wilderness was designated, Leopold left New Mexico for Wisconsin. The holistic perspective he espoused in wildlife studies made him a pioneer of what was coming to be called ecology. Leopold's best-known book was a collection of essays entitled *A Sand County Almanac*, published a year after his accidental death in 1948. Here he recorded thoughts and feelings that had stirred him since his youth: protecting that which remains of the wild, the necessity of human experience with the wild, and the belief that love and respect should guide the relationships that human beings have with the lands they inhabit.

In looking both backward and forward from Leopold's time, it is clear that in the course of what we call western civilization, the term "wilderness" has usually connoted places that threatened danger or desolation, places that were to be avoided, or better, to be eliminated and brought to the service of man. The nineteenth-century westward expansion of the United States was a long, drawn-out example of such struggle and shaping. Changes in people's attitudes began near the century's end, however, and in another generation or two, Aldo Leopold was working out new notions of preserving wild lands—in the contexts of wildlife management, national-forest land, and that which is good for the soul.

Followers of Leopold's vision after his death began a nation-wide campaign for recognition and designation of wilderness areas on the model of the Gila Wilderness. Their efforts culminated in the Wilderness Act of 1964, which gave statutory protection to the Gila and the few other wilderness areas already designated by the Forest Service, and created a review process for identifying additional areas within the national forests, national parks, and national wildlife refuges. Other landmark legislation on behalf of wilderness followed. By the start of the twenty-first century, more than six hundred wilderness areas had been designated, mostly in the West. Twenty-one such areas are in New Mexico, including a large wilderness area adjacent to the Gila that is named for Aldo Leopold.

≈　≈　≈　≈

During most of Aldo Leopold's time in Albuquerque, 1913 to 1924, he and his wife lived in a modest home on South Fourteenth Street. Their back porch looked toward the Rio Grande, not a half-mile away, and between the backyard garden and the marshes of the river stretched an open expanse of grass and brush, rich in birds and small mammals. Here Leopold often wandered with his young children to show them the small wonders of nature.

That undeveloped land at the edge of town has long since given way to streets, homes, and a country-club golf course, as have many other natural areas of New Mexico and elsewhere. Nevertheless, many spectacular and beautiful wild places remain in the Land of Enchantment. Here the glories of open land, azure skies, and far horizons are yet unsullied. Here mountains yet rise in shadowed and sun-bright majesty, cliffs and canyons yet tower and plunge, deserts yet shimmer to the horizons, and grasslands yet wave their bounties beneath drifting clouds.

May it be thus forever.

International Standard Book Number: 1-56579-443-5

Preface, contemporary photography, captions: William A. Stone, ©2003. All rights reserved.
Essays, Afterword: Jerold G. Widdison, ©2003. All rights reserved.

Banner photography on pages 2, 5, 18, 60, 86, 103, 125, and 154: © 2001, Gordon and Cathie Sullivan. Used by permission.

Photographs protected by other copyrights are noted with the images; text passages protected by other copyrights are noted on this page.

Editor: Martha Ripley Gray
Production: Carol Pando
Production Manager: Craig Keyzer

Publisher:
Westcliffe Publishers, Inc., P.O. Box 1261, Englewood, CO 80150
westcliffepublishers.com

Printed in China by C & C Offset Printing, Ltd.

No portion of this book, either text or photography, may be reproduced in any form, including electronically, without the express written permission of the publisher.

Library of Congress Cataloging-in-Publication Data

Stone, William A.
New Mexico : then & now / contemporary rephotography by William Stone ; preface by William Stone ; essays and afterword by Jerold Widdison.
p. cm.
Includes bibliographical references.
ISBN 1-56579-443-5
1. New Mexico--Pictorial works. 2. New Mexico--History--Pictorial works. 3. New Mexico--History, Local--Pictorial works. 4. Landscape--New Mexico--Pictorial works. I. Title: New Mexico then and now. II. Widdison, Jerold G. III. Title.

F797.S86 2003
978.9'0022'2--dc21 2003052531

*For more information about other fine books and calendars from Westcliffe Publishers, please contact your local bookstore, call us at 1-800-523-3692, write for our free color catalog, or visit us on the Web at **westcliffepublishers.com**.*

ABOUT THE PHOTOGRAPHER

William Stone developed an appreciation for the natural environment while growing up on the coast of New England. After living in various parts of the country, he settled in New Mexico in 1989. Stone specializes in photographing the landscape and ancient cultural sites of the American Southwest. His work has appeared in numerous exhibitions and publications, including two other books from Westcliffe Publishers, *Along New Mexico's Continental Divide Trail* and *New Mexico's Continental Divide Trail: The Official Guide*. He earned degrees from Bowdoin College and the Scripps Institution of Oceanography. Stone and his wife, Carolyn, live near the Sandia Mountains in Albuquerque. Visit williamstonephoto.com.

ABOUT THE AUTHOR

Jerold Widdison is a regional planner involved with public and tribal projects throughout the Southwest. During a thirty-year career, he has been instrumental in establishing or developing numerous state and municipal parks. Also known as a geographer and historian, Jerry is active in resource conservation and historic preservation issues, and for several years he was chairman of the Public Lands Interpretive Association. Jerry's articles on historical and outdoor topics have appeared in *New Mexico Magazine, Arizona Highways, The Denver Post*, and the *New Mexico Historical Review*. He has a master's degree in geography from the University of Colorado at Boulder and is a resident of Albuquerque.

ACKNOWLEDGMENTS

I thank my wife, Carolyn, for her love and encouragement and—when she wasn't helping me find photo locations—for holding down the fort during my frequent absences. I appreciate the enthusiastic support of my parents, Helen and Ed Stone. Jerry Widdison wrote a finely crafted text and generously shared with me his impressive knowledge of New Mexico. Working with the staff of Westcliffe Publishers was a pleasure. I thank John Fielder, Tom Till, Steve Terrill, Joe McGregor, Ray Turner, Steve Donahue, the New Mexico Bureau of Geology & Mineral Resources, the New Mexico Museum of Natural History and Science, White Sands Missile Range, the many property owners who provided access to photo locations, and others who helped along the way. Thanks also to the following authors for generously giving permission to use copyrighted material: Sam Abell for an excerpt from *Sam Abell: The Photographic Life*, © 2002, Rizzoli International Publications; Scott Thybony for an excerpt from *Burntwater*, © 1997, University of Arizona Press; and Charis Wilson for an excerpt from *California and the West*, © 1940 and 1968, Aperture. Finally, I thank the early-day photographers—known and unknown—who so skillfully pictured New Mexico. They made this project possible.

—*William Stone*

BIBLIOGRAPHY

Coke, Van Deren. *Photography in New Mexico*. Albuquerque: University of New Mexico Press, 1979.

Jenkins, Myra E., and Albert H. Schroeder. *A Brief History of New Mexico*. Albuquerque: University of New Mexico Press, 1974.

Johnson, Byron A., ed., with Robert K. Dauner. *Early Albuquerque: A Photographic History, 1870–1918*. Albuquerque: City of Albuquerque, Albuquerque Journal, and Albuquerque Museum, 1981.

Julyan, Robert. *The Place Names of New Mexico*. Albuquerque: University of New Mexico Press, 1996.

Klett, Mark, et al. *Second View: The Rephotographic Survey Project*. Albuquerque: University of New Mexico Press, 1984.

Newhall, Beaumont, and Diana E. Edkins. *William H. Jackson*. Dobbs Ferry, N.Y.: Morgan & Morgan, 1974.

Simmons, Marc. *New Mexico: An Interpretive History*. Albuquerque: University of New Mexico Press, 1988.

HISTORIC PHOTO CREDITS

Historic photographs were graciously provided by the following sources: Albuquerque Museum; American Museum of Natural History; Amon Carter Museum; Artesia Historical Museum & Art Center; Aztec Museum; Bureau of Land Management; Center for Creative Photography; Colorado Historical Society; Colorado Railroad Museum; Richard Dean; Deming-Luna Mimbres Museum; Denver Public Library Western History Department; Farmington Museum; Geronimo Springs Museum; Historical Society for Southeast New Mexico; Joseph Edward Smith Photography Museum and Gallery; Library of Congress; Lincoln County Historical Society; Los Alamos Historical Society; Missouri Historical Society; Museum of New Mexico; National Archives; National Geodetic Survey; New Mexico State University Library–Rio Grande Historical Collections; Raton Museum; Sacramento Mountains Historical Society; Silver City Museum; Southeastern New Mexico Historical Society of Carlsbad; Tularosa Basin Historical Society; Union County Historical Society–Herzstein Memorial Museum; U.S. Bureau of Reclamation; U.S. Forest Service; and U.S. Geological Survey.

Note: The Joseph Edward Smith Photography Museum and Gallery in Socorro, New Mexico, established in 2003, is the former home and studio of Joe E. Smith, territorial photographer. For information about the Museum, or to order prints, please contact Suzanne Smith, P.O. Box GG, Socorro, NM 87801.

Page #	*Photo Credit*
2	Library of Congress
4	Colorado Historical Society
5	(Plaza) Museum of New Mexico neg #11329 (capitol) Museum of New Mexico neg #10372
6	(cathedral) Museum of New Mexico neg #131794 (Santa Fe) Museum of New Mexico neg #10173
7	Museum of New Mexico neg #45819
8	National Archives
10	Museum of New Mexico neg #10392
11	Museum of New Mexico neg #10059
12	National Archives
13	National Archives
14	Museum of New Mexico neg #10685
16	Museum of New Mexico neg #11047
17	Museum of New Mexico neg #11125
18	(Taos Pueblo) National Archives (lumber) U.S. Forest Service
19	Museum of New Mexico neg #516
20	U.S. Geological Survey
22	(both) Colorado Historical Society
23	Colorado Railroad Museum Collection
24	Museum of New Mexico neg #15574
25	Museum of New Mexico neg #16523
26	Colorado Historical Society
28	Denver Public Library Western History Department
29	Colorado Historical Society
30	Museum of New Mexico neg #13751
31	Museum of New Mexico neg #13754
32	Colorado Historical Society
34	Museum of New Mexico neg #39350
36	Museum of New Mexico neg #36466
37	Denver Public Library Western History Department
38	Museum of New Mexico neg #4432
40	Museum of New Mexico neg #86282
41	U.S. Forest Service
42	Museum of New Mexico neg #148833
43	Museum of New Mexico neg #11592
44	(fire department) Albuquerque Museum #1978.141.102 (Hodgin) Albuquerque Museum neg #1980.159.012
45	Museum of New Mexico neg #15139
46	Museum of New Mexico neg #14570
47	Albuquerque Museum #1978.050.716
48	Colorado Historical Society
50	Albuquerque Museum #1980.020.002
51	Albuquerque Museum #1978.050.036
52	Museum of New Mexico neg #8600
53	Missouri Historical Society
54	Missouri Historical Society
56	Museum of New Mexico neg #51466
58	Collection Center for Creative Photography, University of Arizona, ©1981 Arizona Board of Regents
59	U.S. Geological Survey
60	Aztec Museum
61	U.S. Geological Survey
62	Bureau of Land Management
64	Museum of New Mexico neg #89512
66	Farmington Museum: from the Bob Furman Collection
67	Aztec Museum
68	Colorado Historical Society
69	U.S. Geological Survey
70	American Museum of Natural History #412026
72	Museum of New Mexico neg #6153
73	U.S. Geological Survey
74	U.S. Geological Survey
75	U.S. Geological Survey
76	U.S. Geological Survey
78	U.S. Geological Survey
80	U.S. Geological Survey
82	U.S. Geological Survey
83	Museum of New Mexico neg #15757
84	(Inscription Rock) National Archives (inscription) U.S. Geological Survey
85	U.S. Geological Survey
86	Union County Historical Society–Herzstein Memorial Museum
87	Museum of New Mexico neg #76053
88	Museum of New Mexico neg #9556
89	Museum of New Mexico neg #51445
90	Museum of New Mexico neg #40589
92	Missouri Historical Society
93	Missouri Historical Society
94	Colorado Historical Society
96	Museum of New Mexico neg #51672
98	Museum of New Mexico neg #1835
99	Museum of New Mexico neg #38212
100	Museum of New Mexico neg #161180
101	Raton Museum
102	U.S. Geological Survey
103	Southeastern New Mexico Historical Society of Carlsbad
104	Museum of New Mexico neg #66012
105	Museum of New Mexico neg #76100
106	Los Alamos Historical Society
108	Los Alamos Historical Society
109	Historical Society for Southeast New Mexico
110	New Mexico State University Library–Rio Grande Historical Collections; Lincoln County Historical Society
112	U.S. Forest Service
114	P1979.223.375 - Laura Gilpin, *White Sands*, November 1945, safety negative ©1979 Amon Carter Museum, Fort Worth, TX, Bequest of the Artist
115	Museum of New Mexico neg #160764
116	Tularosa Basin Historical Society
117	Sacramento Mountains Historical Society
118	U.S. Geological Survey
120	Artesia Historical Museum & Art Center, Mathis Family Collection
121	Southeastern New Mexico Historical Society of Carlsbad
122	Museum of New Mexico neg #52059
124	Southeastern New Mexico Historical Society of Carlsbad
125	U.S. Geological Survey
126	U.S. Geological Survey
127	National Archives
128	Museum of New Mexico neg #5802
129	Richard Dean
130	National Geodetic Survey
131	New Mexico State University Library Rio Grande Historical Collections
132	New Mexico State University Library Rio Grande Historical Collections
134	Museum of New Mexico neg #5234
135	Museum of New Mexico neg #13781
136	Museum of New Mexico neg # 1742
137	Colorado Historical Society
138	Deming-Luna Mimbres Museum
140	Museum of New Mexico neg #76124
141	Museum of New Mexico neg #13780
142	Geronimo Springs Museum
144	U.S. Bureau of Reclamation
146	Museum of New Mexico neg #11400
147	Silver City Museum
148	U.S. Geological Survey
150	© J. E. Smith Collection
152	Museum of New Mexico neg #14805
153	© J. E. Smith Collection
154	U.S. Geological Survey